ARCO

50

things

you can do

to get into the

college

of your choice

o'neal Turner, ph.d.

Macmillan • USA

Macmillan • USA
A Simon & Schuster Macmillan Company
1633 Broadway
New York, NY 10019-6785

An ARCO Book

Manufactured in the United States of America

10 9 8 7 6 5 4 3 2 1

Library of Congress Catalog Card Number: 97-071494

ISBN: 0-02-861839-4

Book Design by Nick Anderson

THIS BOOK IS DEDICATED TO MY VARIOUS FAMILIES:

My immediate family—Debbie, O'Neal ("Best Guy"), and Ashley ("Princess")

My extended family of Turners, Froles, Schaefers, and Vignals

My family at The Culver Academies

My family of colleagues, both high school counselors and college admission professionals

contents

Part Three Making Your Choice

introduction

Getting into college is not an easy task. In fact, many would agree that getting into the college of your choice is more difficult today than ever before.

The primary purpose of this book is to provide a list of 50 "Things" that you can do to improve your chances of getting into your dream school. Individually these items may not seem important, but collectively they pack a powerful admission punch.

Some "Things" are very obvious, such as "#1—Select the Right Courses in High School" or "#2—Keep Your Grades Up All Through High School." Others may strike you as a bit unusual. I can assure you that all will have an impact.

For the sake of specific directions, each "Thing" is divided into three areas:

1. Why Do It

2. How to Do It

3. What You'll Get Out of It

In addition to these 50 "Things," I have included information to guide you through "The College Exploration Process." Once you have gained admission to a variety of colleges, you might find the section "Selecting the 'Best' College Option" helpful in making your final college choice. Finally, in the section "Author's Choice," I share some opinions about where to find particularly strong college majors and special features as well as my own favorite colleges by geographical location.

I hope you find this book a welcome guide as you attempt to gain admission to the college of your choice.

about the author

O'NEAL TURNER, PH.D., has been active in the field of education since his graduation from college. At the secondary level, he has been a teacher, director of college counseling, and independent college counselor. At the collegiate level, he has worked in admission offices at Colby College and Georgetown University. He was Director of Admission at Ohio Wesleyan University and Dean of Admission at Butler University. Dr. Turner is currently the Dean of Enrollment Management and College Advising at The Culver Academies, in Culver, Indiana.

He received his B.A. from Dartmouth College, M.A. from Loyola Marymount University, and Ph.D. from the American University. He is currently pursuing his Master of Science in Administration from the University of Notre Dame.

part one

starting *your* search

the college

exploration *process*

With so many colleges to choose from, how do you find the one that's right for you? You start by creating a college exploration plan.

This chapter shows you how to create a manageable plan that you can follow. The plan has seven parts.

Turner's 7-Step College Search Plan

1. Define college features that are important to you.
2. Create a list of colleges that have the features you select.
3. Gather information from and about these colleges.
4. Establish a list that includes a wide range of colleges based on admission criteria.
5. Explore these colleges, preferably firsthand.
6. Modify your college list based on your exploration.
7. Apply to a range of colleges.

---

1. Define college features that are important to you.

Before you can find and apply to the colleges you like best, you'll need to decide which features are most important to you and then see which colleges have the features you want.

To begin your exploration, you need to concentrate on seven areas of concern. As you examine each area, you will learn which characteristics are truly important to you, and this knowledge will help guide you toward colleges that are excellent choices.

Here are the areas you need to examine to determine which colleges you should explore:

1. Academic issues
2. Admission issues
3. College features
4. Financial features
5. After-college issues
6. Policy issues
7. Other issues

Academic Issues

Academic issues include various aspects of the college's learning environment. Depending on your goals and your learning style, some of these issues may be of vital importance to you:

- *Atmosphere.* Is the scholastic atmosphere rigorous, demanding, relatively easy, easy, or ridiculously easy?
- *Programs.* Does the college offer particular majors or programs of interest to you?
- *Advising system.* How is the academic advising system (faculty members who give advice on your course selection, curriculum counselors, and so on) set up at this college?
- *Class size.* What is the average size of classes taken in the freshman year? What are the average sizes of classes taken in the sophomore, junior, and senior years?
- *Off-campus study opportunities.* Does this college have arrangements with other institutions so that students may also enroll at other colleges?
- *Student-faculty relations.* How much, and how often, do students and faculty interact, both inside and outside class?

Admission Issues

Admission issues focus on how you apply to a specific college and how your application is judged for admission to the college. Consider the following:

- *Admission criteria.* What are the college's specific requirements (standards for admission) for grades, class rank, SAT I and II scores, and ACT scores?
- *Financial aid considerations.* Does the admission office view candidates differently based on their need for financial assistance?
- *Application deadline.* When do you have to apply, and when do you learn of the admission decision?
- *Family relationships with the college.* Do you have any family connection to the college? Did your father or mother, siblings, or grandparents attend? A family tradition at a college may influence your decision.

College Features

These issues have an impact on the quality of life on campus:

- *Campus setting.* What are the primary features of the setting of the campus (park-like, rural, or city-like)? What are the advantages and disadvantages of each setting?
- *Competition level.* Is the general "feel" of the campus described as very competitive, competitive, or noncompetitive in a variety of areas other than academic, such as social life or intramural activities?
- *Safety.* What are the statistics for crime on campus? What are the most common types of crime on campus? Are there any trends in crime on campus?
- *Diversity.* What is the gender, ethnic, economic, social, and geographic diversity of the student body, administration, and faculty?
- *Facilities.* What shape are the campus facilities in? What are the newest and most recently refurbished buildings on campus? What is the building plan over the next few years?
- *Social life.* How do students describe the social life on campus? What social activities are sponsored by the college or by on-campus groups? Do students remain on campus on the weekends, or do they leave campus?

Financial Features

Finances include not only the cost of the education, but also the college's policy of distributing resources. Consider these financial features:

- *Cost.* What is the *total* cost of the college—tuition, room, board, books, fees, supplies, transportation, and miscellaneous?
- *Scholarships.* What scholarships are available, and what are the criteria for awarding them? How do the criteria change from year to year?
- *Loans.* What types and terms of loans are available through the college or other sources?
- *Policy.* Does the college award resources to meet the full financial "need" of candidates?

After-College Issues

Graduate school, career opportunities, and networking options can all play a role in a graduate's life *after* college. Consider the following issues:

- *Alumni.* How financially and enthusiastically supportive are the graduates of the college? What type(s) of employment networking programs exist at the college?
- *Career services.* What types of career services are offered to the student body, and when?
- *Job opportunities.* Does the college provide extensive information about job opportunities? What percent of last spring's graduates were employed by the following September? How many graduates use the career-services office? What are some of the companies that frequently employ graduates?
- *Graduate schools.* What percent of students apply and are admitted to graduate schools by the time of graduation? What are the graduate schools most often applied to and admitted to? What percent of students apply and are admitted to graduate schools within two years of graduation?

Policy Issues

The regulations imposed by a college indicate a great deal about the mission and philosophy of the school. The same policies can either simplify or complicate student life. They include:

- *Religious requirements.* What are the requirements for religious classes or observation by the students?
- *Honor system.* Does the college have an honor code or system? What are the requirements?

- *Dress code.* What is the dress code, if any?
- *Student behavior.* What are the requirements for student behavior? What are the alcohol and drug policies on campus? How are these policies enforced?

Other Issues

These issues don't quite fit into any of the other categories but might be important considerations for selecting colleges:

- *Endowment.* What was the size of the college's endowment last year compared to the preceding year? What percent of the endowment is being used for college budgets?
- *Freshmen attrition.* What percent of the freshmen return for their sophomore year?
- *Upper-class retention.* What percent of the students graduate in four years? What percent take five or more years?
- *Weather.* What's the weather like during the regular school year? Are you looking for variety or consistency?

2. CREATE A LIST OF COLLEGES THAT HAVE THE FEATURES YOU SELECT.

Once you have examined each of the seven areas of concern, you are ready to select the ones that are most important to you. Make a list of these issues and use them as signposts to find the colleges that are the best "fits" for you.

The next logical question you might ask is this: "Now that I have opinions about particular college-related issues, how do I find the colleges that have the features that are most important to me?" Good question!

There are many people you can turn to for names of colleges that might be good matches for you. These people include:

- *High school friends.* Many of your friends are conducting their own search. Share opinions and information with each other.
- *Family members.* These people know you well and might have some insights about your personality traits.
- *Current college students.* These people are already doing what you want to do—going to college. Listen to what they have to say about their search for the right college.

- *College graduates.* While some of these people might say, "Been there, done that," recent graduates can provide insights that may be helpful.
- *High school teachers.* These folks deal with students all the time. They might just have some perspectives that would prove valuable.
- *High school counselors.* These professionals are the most familiar with matching schools and students. Listen carefully to what these advisors have to say.

3. GATHER INFORMATION FROM AND ABOUT COLLEGES.

Take the names of those colleges suggested to you by others and do some research on your own. Start by exploring one or more of the best-selling college guides. Generally speaking, there are two types of college guides. One is objective, providing only statistical information such as enrollment figures, gender statistics, class size, expenses, academic majors, and admission criteria. Although there are dozens of guides available, I highly recommend these objective texts:

- Barron's *Profiles of American Colleges*
- The College Board's *The College Handbook*
- Lovejoy's *College Guide*
- Peterson's *Guide to Four-Year Colleges*

The other type of college guide is more subjective, offering the opinions of reviewers and/or students currently attending the particular college. Typically, these guides are compiled from surveys that are distributed to students attending these colleges. A reviewer molds the description of each school from the survey results. The areas discussed include best majors, majors to avoid, academic atmosphere, dating environment, best and worst residential facilities, and job opportunities. In recent years, a number of these books have been published. Some are viewed as more serious and reliable than others. I recommend the following:

- *The Selective Guide to Colleges,* by Edward Fiske
- *The Insider's Guide to the Colleges,* by the Editors of the *Yale Daily News*
- *The Princeton Review Guide to the 310 Best Colleges in America*
- *The 100 Best Colleges for African-American Students,* by Erlene Wilson

Both objective and subjective college guides are excellent sources for "checking out" colleges that have been recommended by others, and for discovering new college possibilities on your own.

After you have read *about* the colleges, your next step is to call or write and request information *from* the colleges that interest you. Remember, though, that all of the information sent by the colleges is really advertising, designed to present each school in the best possible light. Most colleges have these resources available:

- Viewbooks—pictorial information about the school
- Visitor guides—map, directions, and lodging information
- Course catalogs—a listing of all classes taught at the college
- Videotape or CD-ROM—everything mentioned above

Examining these sources of information about and from the colleges will help you finalize the list of colleges you will explore.

4. ESTABLISH A LIST THAT INCLUDES A WIDE RANGE OF COLLEGES BASED ON ADMISSION CRITERIA.

Once you have a list of colleges that both meet your "features" criteria and excite your interest, it's time to categorize these colleges based on your chance of admission.

Using the college's admission requirements found in both the material about and from the colleges, as well as your academic and standardized test performance to date, you will be able to determine whether the odds of your being offered admission are good, average, or a long shot. Once you have determined which colleges fall into which group, make sure you have at least three schools in each category.

Your high school counselor will probably have a record of the students from your school who have applied to the colleges on your list. Your counselor can also help you place the schools you have chosen into the "Reach," "Ballpark," and "Looks Good" categories:

- *"Reach" schools.* These are colleges where you have less than a 50 percent chance of gaining admission. You need to weigh the value of applying to these colleges. While you might be disappointed if you don't gain admission, you will never know unless you apply.

- *"Ballpark" schools.* These are colleges where you have a 50–50 chance of admission. For example, if you apply to four ballpark colleges, you will probably gain admission to two.
- *"Looks Good" schools.* These are colleges where you have better than a 50 percent chance of gaining admission. While you might be much less excited about these colleges than you are about those in the other two categories, you should still be happy to enroll in them if they are your only options.

Once you have chosen colleges (at least three) in each of the three categories, you are ready to check them out personally. That way, you will both narrow down your list and confirm those colleges that are excellent choices for your next four years.

5. EXPLORE THESE COLLEGES, PREFERABLY FIRSTHAND.

The best way to determine whether a specific college is a good match for you is to visit it. To use a popular analogy, you wouldn't buy a $40,000 car without test-driving it, so why would you choose to attend a $50,000–$150,000 college without first visiting it?

Equally important, some admission directors believe that a greater percentage of students who visit will enroll. Since colleges are competing for students, many admission directors view in a more favorable light the applications of students who have visited the campus.

Tips for a Successful Campus Visit

1. Plan for your trip at least two weeks in advance.
2. Budget your time—allow a minimum of four hours on campus.
3. Schedule by phone; conflicts are more easily handled by phone than mail.
4. Have a date and time in mind; weekdays are best, but be flexible.
5. Meet with as many people as you can, such as financial aid counselors, coaches, faculty, etc.
6. Choose a personal interview rather than a group session if possible.
7. Get names—from the person scheduling your visit to the interviewer.
8. Request written confirmation of your scheduled appointments.

Group Session or Personal Interview

While a few colleges offer you the option of either a group session or a personal interview, most give you no choice. Though each is different in format, the goal of both is the same: sharing information about the college. Nevertheless, there are things you can do in either situation to further your chances of gaining admission.

The group session is a presentation of the college to students and their families by a member of the admission staff. It typically includes viewing the college video and participating in an extensive question-and-answer period. Aside from this question-and-answer period, there is usually no contact with the admission staff. Generally, the group session is offered at medium- and larger-sized colleges.

The personal interview is a discussion between you and an admission representative. This is an outstanding way not only for you to learn a great deal about the college, but also for the interviewer to learn about you. In many cases, the interviewer evaluates you by the presentation of your academic record and extracurricular activities, by your personality, and by your preparedness. The personal interview is generally offered by smaller colleges.

Campus Tour

The tour of the campus is nothing less than a moving sales pitch. From the route taken across campus, to the comments made (or not made) by your guide, from the answers to your questions, to even the clothing of the guide, everything is scripted, packaged, and polished by the admission office. If you recognize the sales aspect of the tour, you already have one-half of a great tour—that is, the proper attitude. The other half centers on knowing what to look for, knowing what to ask, and knowing where to revisit during your "walkaround" after the tour.

6. MODIFY YOUR COLLEGE LIST BASED ON YOUR EXPLORATION.

After completing your college visits, you'll want to think about what you've learned and make some important decisions. I strongly suggest you do the following:

- Find a quiet place and ask yourself some important questions:
  What did I like best/least about each college?
  What words come to my mind when I remember my visit to each school?
  What words come to my mind when I describe each college?
- Discuss your visit with your parents or any friend who may have accompanied you and ask questions like these:
  What did you like best/least about each college?
  What words come to mind when you remember your visit to each school?
  What words come to mind when you describe each college?
- Discuss your views about your visit with those whose opinions you respect.
- Return to that quiet place, review all you have seen and heard, examine your true feelings about each school, and then decide:
  Where do you want to apply to college?
  Specifically, why do you want to apply to these colleges?

7. APPLY TO A RANGE OF COLLEGES.

After thoughtfully considering many colleges, you must make one final decision—namely, applying to a wide range of colleges.

This is the point at which some students make some tragic mistakes. Here are the three most common:

1. *Applying to only one or two colleges.* Although you can attend only one school, you want to leave yourself options.
2. *Applying to 15–20 colleges.* The application process alone will take too much time away from your academic work. You'll do a better job on your applications—and your school work—if you narrow down the field.
3. *Applying to colleges in only one or two of the ranges—Reach, Ballpark, or Looks Good.* If you select at least two schools in each range, you are more likely to have a variety of college admission options—and all of the options will be acceptable to you.

SUMMARY

By using this seven-step search plan, you will have thoroughly examined your interests, created an initial college list that meets your academic and personal needs, visited these colleges, and determined your final application list to maximize your chances of getting into the college of your choice.

part two

50 things

you can do

to get into the

college

of your choice

freshman
year *in*
high school

#1—Select the Right Courses in High School

Why Do It

Most people think the freshman year is a bit early for students to plan their entire high school program. On the one hand, the freshman year *is* too early. You're still trying to figure out where your classes are held and when you can eat lunch. On the other hand, if you're planning to go on to college, you need to know the "minimum" high school requirements for the colleges you are considering.

There are five major subject areas that are the building blocks of a good educational foundation: English, foreign language, math, natural sciences, and social sciences. The more years of these subjects you take in high school (with good grades, of course), the better prepared you will be for admission to the most selective colleges.

How to Do It

The following shows three different high school programs. These samples represent the requirements of a variety of colleges from least selective to most selective. Choose the program that is most representative of the type of college you hope to attend (aim high). Share your hopes with your high school counselor, who can guide you in selecting the courses you need for the colleges of your choice.

Many colleges have these "minimum" high school requirements:

English	4 years
Foreign language (one language)	2 years
Math (algebra 1, geometry)	3 years
Natural sciences (intro. science, biology)	3 years
Social sciences	3 years
Total	**15 years**

Here are the high school requirements for "selective colleges":

English	4 years
Foreign language (one language)	3 years
Math (algebra 1, geometry, algebra 2)	3 years
Natural sciences (biology, chemistry, physics)	3 years
Social sciences	3 years
Total	**16 years**

The high school requirements for the "most selective colleges" are known as the "Magic 20." These colleges expect their students to nearly exhaust the subject areas *and* accelerated levels (Advanced Placement, Honors, or Enriched) of those courses. An example of this course selection includes:

English	4 years
Foreign language (one language)	4 years
Math (algebra 1, geometry, algebra 2, advanced math)	4 years
Natural sciences	4 years
Social sciences	4 years
Total	**20 years**

What You'll Get Out of It

Let's pretend you could meet with the deans of admission at the most selective colleges in the country. During your meeting with them, you ask, "What are the two most important areas you focus on when reviewing an application?" I'll bet you my University of Notre Dame football season tickets that all would have the same answer: "Demanding courses with strong grades."

If you have not taken the right courses in high school, it is very difficult to convince a college admission representative that you are prepared to do excellent work at a very demanding college. However, if you have performed well in difficult high school courses, you can demonstrate your readiness to do good work at a demanding college.

#2—Keep Your Grades Up All Through High School

Why Do It

If earning good grades in tough courses is the single most important thing you can do to get into the colleges to which you apply, it makes sense to say that the better you perform in high school, the more college options you'll have.

While it may be true that college admission officers admire students who have had a slow start academically and then "turn it around" after a year or so, these same admission officers generally admit to their colleges those students who have started, continued, and finished high school with excellent grades.

Your goal should be to focus on doing your best in the most challenging courses right from the start. Students who center on this goal are usually the same students who are delighted and proud when college decisions are announced in their senior year.

How to Do It

It's easy to say that earning good grades in high school is important. It certainly is much more difficult to do it. Over my many years as a student and teacher, I have found certain strategies help me and my students earn good grades. While some of these things might be a bit obvious, others might be new to you and worth a try.

Turner's Top 10 Tips for Better Grades

10. *Establish a daily schedule.* Don't worry about scheduling every spare minute, but try to set aside time each day for sleep, learning, exercise, social activities, personal needs, and laughter. The "learning" time is both in class and study time.

9. *Find a comfortable place to study.* The best place to study is one where you can concentrate on your work without falling asleep. Your bedroom may be nice and quiet, but your bed is probably *not* a good place to study.

8. *Prepare for each class.* Spend a few moments each evening to review your work in each class. It won't take long, but it will help you shine for that "pop quiz" or when you're called on by the teacher.

7. *Highlight as you read.* When you read, highlight those points/ issues/dates/names in the book that have been emphasized in class. It isn't enough to just read the assignment; you have to get a handle on the key elements and understand their relationship to the material presented in class.

6. *Learn how to take good class notes.* The ability to take good notes in class is critical to learning. If you can't do this well, find someone who can help you learn this vital skill.

5. *Review and rewrite your notes the same day.* Although this may sound a bit drastic, I strongly recommend that you set aside time each day to rewrite or review your notes from class while they are still fresh in your mind.

4. *Work in groups.* Talk about your courses with your classmates. A friend may be able to explain a point you didn't quite understand. In addition, a group of friends might make a great study group. Just make certain that you actually spend time studying.

3. *Take a break.* It is always wise to take an occasional break when studying (15 minutes every couple of hours should do). If you find yourself in a particular "groove," then keep going, but most of us need to pause every now and then.

2. *Pace yourself.* Don't look at a big project and view it as impossible. On the other hand, don't leave work until the last minute. Take a good, long look at your work and make a plan that lets you complete it in small, steady steps. The secret is to keep going.

1. *Believe in yourself.* One of my favorite quotes is from the movie *A League of Their Own*. Tom Hanks, as the team's manager, tells a player, "Of course it's hard, it's supposed to be hard. If it wasn't hard, everyone would do it. It's the hard that makes it great." You can do well in high school. Plan ahead, work at it daily, and rebound when you get frustrated. If you follow these steps, you'll do fine.

What You'll Get Out of It

It is one thing to *hope* you earn good grades in high school. It is something else to create a plan to earn those grades and stick to it.

Turner's Top 10 Tips are designed to help you use your ability to earn the best grades possible. Earning those grades will open many college admission doors for you.

#3—Explore Extracurricular Activities at School

Why Do It

You may have heard the expression "All work and no play makes Jack (or Jill) a dull person." Well, it's true. Colleges are interested in admitting well-rounded human beings who have more than just one interest. To that end, college admission officers would like to know how you contribute to your school other than as a student in the classroom.

Most college applications ask you to list your extracurricular activities. Colleges do this for two reasons. One, admission officers are genuinely interested in "getting to know you" both in and outside the classroom. Two, colleges are communities with numerous activities for students. These activities may include fine and performing arts, athletics, publications, student government, and clubs. In order to maintain these activities, colleges want and need students who have demonstrated ability and interest in these activities. The best way to find these students is to use the application to ask applicants about their interests.

Many colleges care deeply about the talents and skills of their applicants. Most college admission offices make sure that these skills are evaluated and counted when considering an application to college.

If all things are equal (courses, grades, scores), a college admission officer may value more a student with extensive and focused extracurricular activities, than a student who has few activities. Without question, these activities help your efforts to gain admission.

How to Do It

Give this some serious thought. Find a few activities (one to three) you would like to explore. It's wise not to become too involved as a freshman. You don't want your grades to suffer because of "over" activity. Try to find a balance between getting involved in a couple of activities and earning good grades.

When deciding which activities to explore, follow these five steps:

1. Don't be afraid to explore new activities—those you know nothing about.
2. Ask certain questions about each activity:
   - How much time is required each week?
   - When is the "busy" time during the year?

- Is this is a "freshmen friendly" activity?
- How many other freshmen are involved?

3. Find a friend to join the activity with you. While this should not be a criterion for joining a particular activity, it makes the "joining" easier.

4. Give the activity some time. Even if you don't enjoy the activity at first, give it a few weeks. It's always hard to be the new kid on the block, but the going gets much easier once people get to know you. If you give it time and energy and still don't like it, admit that you have made a mistake and move on to explore other activities.

5. Keeping in mind the balance of academics and activities, get involved. Try to volunteer. An active member is more likely to be welcomed by the group.

Most high schools have a wide variety of extracurricular activities to explore. These activities/clubs might include:

- Fine arts
- Performing arts
  - Vocal
  - Instrumental
  - Theater
- Clubs
  - Language
  - Hobby
  - Career interest
  - Political
- Community service organizations
- Publications
  - Newspaper
  - Yearbook
  - Literary magazine
- Athletics
  - Varsity
  - Junior varsity
  - Intramural
- Student government
- Debate

What You'll Get Out of It

Colleges are communities where learning takes place both in and outside the classroom. One avenue of leaning is through becoming part of a group of people who enjoy a similar activity. College admission officers look for students who have done well in the classroom, but also have made positive contributions in nonacademic areas.

Most college admission officers would say that 5 to 15 percent of the decision to offer admission to a student is based on the student's contribution to his or her high school. Finding a couple of activities during your freshman year and continuing to develop your role in them throughout your high school years might convince an admission officer that you can make a similar positive contribution to the college community.

#4—Develop Interests Outside School

Why Do It

All of us have interests away from school or work. For many of us, these interests or hobbies are an important part of our identity.

In trying to learn whether you would make a welcome member of their community, college admission officers try very hard to get to know you. In addition to your courses, grades, and scores, these officers want to know about your activities in and outside school.

Continuing to develop your hobbies or interests is a great way to share with the college another side of yourself.

How to Do It

Think about yourself when not at school. Aside from "hanging out with friends," what do you enjoy doing? Ask yourself a few questions:

- What do I like to do when not in school?
- Do I collect anything?
- Do friends ask me about a certain subject because they think I know a great deal about it?
- Do I especially enjoy reading about any particular subjects?
- Have I helped, or would I like to help, people in need?

Your answers to these questions might help you find a couple of activities that are especially meaningful to you.

Interests You Might Develop

- Collections
    - Sports cards
    - Coins
    - Stamps
- Reading
    - Anything
    - Particular authors
    - Particular subjects
- Writing
    - Daily journal or diary
    - Short stories

- Sports teams
- Travel
- Part-time job
- Computers
    - Games
    - The Internet
- Community service
- Church or synagogue participation
- Activities
    - Sports
    - Animals

Whatever the activity or interest might be, do not feel you must give it up once you are in high school. On the contrary, you should keep up your interests and develop them even further.

What You'll Get Out of It

I will never forget a question one parent asked me during a college admission seminar. After I had explained the importance college admission officers place on the hobbies of applicants, a well-meaning mother asked, "So which hobbies are most important to colleges?" I responded that there was no order of importance for hobbies. Rather, I emphasized that colleges are simply interested in learning what students do with their time away from school.

By sharing your hobbies and what they mean to you, you give colleges a clearer picture of the person you are. Those students who present a more complete picture of themselves to the colleges are more likely to attract the attention of admission officers.

#5—Read and Write Every Day

Why Do It

It is impossible to think that a student can excel in high school without reading and writing. I am not referring to assigned reading and writing, but rather to the reading and writing that students do on their own.

Getting into the habit of writing in a journal every day or reading something you have chosen to explore can pay major benefits in many ways, such as:

- expanding your knowledge of a particular subject
- enhancing a hobby or interest
- expanding your vocabulary
- providing insight into yourself
- developing a lifetime skill
- refreshing and invigorating your life
- adding some fun to your day

How to Do It

For reading, just find a subject, period of history, or author or poet who interests you and read. If possible, set aside a few minutes each day (many prefer early morning or just before going to sleep) to read a few pages. You might just be amazed at the:

- knowledge you acquire
- ease with which you are led to other topics or authors
- loyalty you acquire to a particular author or poet

Most students are afraid to put pen to paper and write. The best way to overcome this fear is to get into the habit of keeping a journal or diary. Write in your journal every day for a week; then reread what you have written. You'll probably be amazed at how quickly you get used to putting your feelings on paper. You might also be impressed with your:

- writing style
- knack for words
- honesty
- enthusiasm for putting your fears and hopes into words

What You'll Get Out of It

Many educators would agree that two skills in short supply among high school students today are reading and writing skills. Your freshman year of high school is the ideal time to start developing these skills in earnest. If you take time to read and write every day, I believe you will be very pleased at what will greet you in the mailbox four years from now: college admission offers from many outstanding colleges. And one of the many reasons these offers of admission will be extended to you is that your reading and writing skills differentiate you from many other talented applicants.

#6—Take Time to Assess Your Progress

Why Do It

Too many high school students jump into the whirlwind of school activities and forget to take time to see how they are doing.

This is an easy trap to fall into when you enter high school. You want to "fit in" (find a group that is accepting of you), you want to get involved, and you want to earn good grades. That's a pretty tall order!

While you are trying to do all of these things, it's important to pause once in a while to see how you are doing. You have to step off the treadmill of high school in order to feel that you have some control over this new experience.

How to Do It

Take a few minutes each week and ask yourself some important questions about how you are doing with this "high school stuff." Although the questions may vary, the general purpose is for you to reflect on yourself and gauge your progress.

Questions You Should Ask Yourself

About Academics

- How am I progressing in my classes?
- What are my strongest/weakest subjects?
- Am I seeking help to improve in my weak subjects?
- Have I done anything "special" for myself when I have done well?
- Am I sharing my successes/problems with my family?

About Extracurricular Activities

- Am I involved in activities I enjoy?
- What do I enjoy/dislike most about my activities?
- Do I have a balance between school and personal activities?

About Relationships

- Have I taken the time to make friends?
- What kind of influences do these friends have on me?
- Is there any one "special" friend?

About Personal Issues
- What am I happiest about in my life right now?
- What would I most like to change in my life?
- What have I learned about myself from my journal/diary?

By asking yourself these questions (and taking the time to answer them), you are allowing yourself to take a look at your progress. This helps you gain some perspective. Instead of thinking only about "doing," you are allowing yourself to reflect on "*how* you are doing."

What You'll Get Out of It

When we think about gaining admission to college, most of us think about courses, grades, activities, and test scores. While these are very important elements in the admission process, they need to be monitored to ensure admission success. It's a good idea to step back periodically to see how you are doing.

This process is similar to buying an expensive car for a long trip but never bothering to consult a map or to check the status of your oil or gas. You may be headed in the right direction, but you need to stop on occasion to make sure of where you are going and to see whether your engine is working well.

The practice of taking time to check your progress is a habit that will serve you well throughout your life. I strongly suggest you make this a weekly habit in high school.

#7—Spend Time with Those Who Care

Why Do It

High school can be a very lonely place for many students, especially freshmen. Everything seems very different and a bit overwhelming. Many students do not know where to turn for security or comfort. As a result, they find it hard to concentrate on getting good grades.

If you have the feeling that you don't belong, don't despair. There are many people you can turn to for support and comfort—people who can help you achieve the goal of being successful in high school.

How to Do It

In order to feel you are supported in this new experience, it is a good idea to think about those people who care most about you. Make a list of these people. Arrange to spend some time each week with some of these people and share with them your hopes and fears.

Your list of people who care might include:

> parents
> siblings
> other family members
> friends
> teachers
> high school counselors
> coaches
> neighbors
> employers

Sharing your fears and hopes with people who care about you has two important results:

1. You feel support and confidence growing in yourself.
2. These people feel a "connection" with you and are pleased you cared enough about them to share your feelings.

In short, both you and they gain something from the experience. They support you, and you honor them. That's a very nice feeling for both of you.

What You'll Get Out of It

The English author John Donne wrote in his famous meditation that "No man is an island, entire of itself; every man is a piece of the continent, a part of the main. . . ." Donne's message is simple but powerful: We are all in this world together, and we need to rely on each other.

Spending time with people who care about you is a great way to receive support and encouragement. For most of us, this kind of support helps us perform at our best. When you excel, you establish and maintain a record that will make any college proud to have you as a member of its community.

#8—Review for the PSAT During the Summer

Why Do It

When deciding whether they will admit you to their college, college admission officers review the results of your standardized tests. The two most important tests are the Scholastic Assessment Test (SAT I and II) and the American College Test (ACT).

To prepare for the SAT I, many students take the Preliminary Scholastic Assessment Test (PSAT) in their *junior* year of high school. The questions on this test are similar to those on SAT I, and students who score especially high on the PSAT are named National Merit Finalists. Many colleges offer admission and hefty scholarships to Finalists.

Rather than wait until the junior year of high school to take the PSAT, I strongly recommend you take the PSAT in October of your *sophomore* year. That way, you have plenty of time to take a long, hard look at your results and take whatever steps are necessary to raise your scores.

How to Do It

To prepare for this important test in October of your sophomore year, I recommend you do some serious preparation during the summer before your sophomore year.

How to Prepare for the PSAT

1. Ask your high school counselor for a copy of the PSAT registration booklet. Study its sample test questions and answers.
2. Go to your local bookstore or library and find a recent study guide to help you learn more about the types of questions on the test and how to answer them.
3. Buy a book with sample tests.
4. Create a weekly study schedule (5–6 hours a week) and stick to it.
5. Take the sample tests and learn from your mistakes.
6. When preparing for this (or any) standardized test, remember these tips:
   - Find a comfortable pace—not too fast or slow.
   - Read each question carefully—know what is being asked.

- Don't "outsmart" the question—give the correct answer.
- Know the directions well—don't waste time reading them.
- Guessing isn't bad—eliminate answers and then guess from what is left.

What You'll Get Out of It

One of best ways to improve your test-taking abilities is to become familiar with the test. Because the PSAT is excellent preparation for the SAT, taking the PSAT in both your sophomore and junior years will help you get your best possible score when it really counts.

sophomore
year *in* high school

#9—Get to Know Graduates of Many Different Colleges

Why Do It

With more than 2,500 four-year colleges in the United States, it's difficult to know much about more than a few of them. One of the most important things you can do to gain admission to colleges is to learn about those colleges that might be best suited to you.

Perhaps the best way to learn about colleges is to talk to people who have been there. Recent graduates are great sources of information about their schools. As you learn about the schools, get to know the graduates as well. Should you decide to apply to their college, they might be willing to put in a good word for you at the admission office.

How to Do It

Take a good look around you and ask this question: "Who do I know that has earned a college degree?" Once you have answered the question, make an appointment to meet with a couple of these people to ask specific questions about their college experiences. The more you learn about their colleges, the better prepared you will be to find the colleges that are the best match for you.

Here are some questions you should ask:

1. When did you start searching for colleges?
   Don't be impressed if the graduate says, "End of my senior year in high school."
2. Who helped you learn about colleges?
   The answer may guide you to another resource.
3. What features were most important to you when exploring colleges?
   The most common answers include:
   - size of the student body
   - distance of the college from home
   - setting of the college (urban, rural, or suburban)
   - cost of the college/availability of financial aid
   - standards of admission/degree of admission difficulty
   - strong academic reputation
   - job/graduate school opportunities after graduation
   - social atmosphere of the campus

4. Which of these features were most important to you when you were attending college, and why?
   Listen carefully to what the graduate thought was important.
5. Which of these features were the least important to you when you were attending college, and why?
6. What should I ask you about college that I have not asked yet?

By asking these questions, you will begin to learn which of the many features of colleges are most important to you. As a result of this new information, you may decide to:

- call the admission office at a few of these colleges and ask to have material mailed to you
- schedule a campus tour so you can take a closer look at some of these colleges

By taking these steps, you not only begin to define your particular college interests, but also learn an important skill—that is, research and exploration.

Another reason for you to meet with graduates of a variety of colleges is that these individuals may be excellent sources of recommendations if and when you decide to apply to their colleges. Imagine how proud a graduate would be to write to the admission office and say, "I am the person responsible for introducing this applicant to my college." While these letters are not written often, when sent, they tend to have a positive impact.

What You'll Get Out of It

Gathering college information from those who have graduated from a particular college is a great way to begin to explore the school. If "information is power," then information from a person who has experienced something firsthand is even more powerful.

With information about a college in one hand, and a recommendation to the college from a graduate in the other, you are increasing your chances of finding an offer of admission in your mailbox during your senior year of high school.

#10—Take the PSAT in October of Your Sophomore Year

Why Do It
The PSAT is an important test for two reasons:

1. It helps prepare you for the SAT, which you will take in your junior and senior years of high school.
2. It is the only test that can qualify you for National Merit status, which is both impressive to college admission offices and financially beneficial to you.

While the sophomore PSAT will not "count" in making you eligible for National Merit status, it is an excellent way to prepare for the test that *will* count: the one you take in October of your junior year.

How to Do It
Because the PSAT "counts" only during the junior year, many high school guidance counselors do not make the PSAT readily available to high school sophomores. Although this may be understandable because of space limitations, it is a roadblock for you, making it difficult to use this opportunity in your sophomore year to prepare for the junior administration of the test.

Therefore, I strongly urge you to approach your counselor in early September of your sophomore year and ask to take the test in October. If necessary, ask your parents to contact your counselor and explain why they want you to take the test in your sophomore *and* your junior years.

Of course, you should have already prepared for this exam by working throughout the summer with different PSAT guidebooks to familiarize yourself with the directions, types of questions, and correct answers. Remember, the better you know the test and the more confident you are in your ability to do well, the better your scores are likely to be.

What You'll Get Out of It
Oddly enough, opening the mail that contains the results of your sophomore PSAT results is a very important moment. If you have done well on the exam, you can approach the administration of the test your junior year with confidence (and with additional preparation). If you have not done well and have the questions and answers, you can determine the

area(s) in which you need to spend more time in preparation for the junior year administration.

Many students psych themselves out of performing well on standardized tests. If you just relax, prepare, take the test, analyze the results, and retake the test, the PSAT, SAT I, SAT II, and ACT would not loom over the college admission horizon as roadblocks to gaining admission to the colleges of your choice.

#11—Get All the Information You Need

Why Do It

It is almost impossible to imagine getting into the colleges that are best for you unless you have spent time exploring a variety of materials from many different sources.

Basically, there are two types of information:

- Information *from* the colleges
- Information *about* the colleges

You need to explore both sources to arrive at your goal: a complete picture of the various types of colleges available.

How to Do It

To get information *from* the college, call, write to, or e-mail the admission office. The information sent may include the following:

- Viewbooks—picture books with literally dozens of handsome photographs
- Departmental literature—brochures describing specific details of a particular academic department
- Visitor guides—brief booklets describing the local accommodations
- Course catalogs—thick books detailing all of the courses, rules, and regulations of each college

Although these materials do help you gain a sense of the place, remember, they are advertisements for the college. Use this information as a starting point, but try to look beyond the glossy pages and check out other sources of information to discover what is really happening on campus.

Generally speaking, there are two types of information *about* the colleges. One consists of *objective* college guides that provide statistical information, such as enrollment figures, admission statistics, gender statistics, and application deadlines. The other includes *subjective* college guides that offer reviews of colleges based on surveys of current students or the observations of outside reviewers. These guides focus on such areas as the best majors on campus, majors to avoid, academic atmosphere, nicest residential facilities, and dating environment. It's a good idea to check both types of sources.

Recommended College Guides

Objective Guides

> Barron's *Profiles of American Colleges*
> The College Board's *The College Handbook*
> Lovejoy's *College Guide*
> Peterson's *Guide to Four-Year Colleges*

Subjective Guides

> *The Selective Guide to Colleges*, by Edward Fiske
> *The Insider's Guide to the Colleges*, by the Editors of the *Yale Daily News*
> *The 100 Best Colleges for African-American Students*, by Erlene Wilson
> *Colleges That Change Lives*, by Loren Pope

What You'll Get Out of It

The key point is that information, whether *from* or *about* colleges, will give you perspective that will help you to decide which colleges are better suited to meet your academic, personal, social, and future needs.

By taking time to explore a wide variety of information, you are gathering the knowledge you need to apply to the colleges that are excellent "fits" for you.

#12—Review and Act On Your Sophomore PSAT Results

Why Do It

If you take the PSAT in October of your sophomore year (suggestion #10), it is critical to review the results as soon as they arrive in your mailbox (in December). Remember, most students don't take this examination until their junior year. Only you, and a few other very intelligent students, have decided to get the jump on the rest of the sophomore class, and you'll want to make the most of your efforts.

Reviewing the results of your PSAT will help you focus on those areas in which you need to improve. By knowing this now, you can address these areas and improve on your PSAT next October or your SAT I later in your sophomore year.

How to Do It

When you get your PSAT results, study them carefully. You want to examine:

- your Selection Index Score
- the results of your performance in particular sections of the test
- your performance compared to both a national and state pool of candidates taking the examination

Remember, this test doesn't count. It won't qualify you for admission to a selective college or eliminate you from consideration for admission; and it won't qualify you for a scholarship grant or eliminate you as a possible recipient. You must wait until December of your junior year for that. However, if you are not pleased with your early PSAT results, you can set to work on improving your score by:

- purchasing and carefully reviewing a book on PSAT review
- taking a course on how to prepare for and take the PSAT
- exploring a computer program on PSAT preparation
- employing the services of a tutor

Although there are no guarantees that your PSAT scores will improve in your junior year, by aggressively and regularly trying to improve your scores, you may be pleased at the results of your junior year PSAT.

What You'll Get Out of It

You have already learned the importance of the PSAT results in terms of college admission and scholarship opportunities. By reviewing the results of the sophomore PSAT, you are addressing any concerns while there is still time to do something about them.

Another very positive result of this aggressive strategy is that you are gaining valuable standardized test-taking skills that will serve you well as you take the PSAT, SAT, and ACT during the next three years.

These testing skills may well improve your test results, thereby strengthening your applications to colleges.

#13—Consider the Sophomore Spring SAT

Why Do It

Having taken the PSAT in October, you are now in a test-taking mode. If you scored fairly high (see your counselor for details), it might be wise to consider the possibility of taking the SAT offered in the spring of your sophomore year. Since most colleges take the highest verbal and math scores from any administration of the test, you will have plenty of additional opportunities to increase your scores. Also, by taking the SAT in your sophomore year, you are becoming familiar with a test that will be very important to your college plans.

How to Do It

The first thing you should do is meet with your high school counselor. Together you should:

- review the results of your sophomore PSAT
- discuss the advantages of taking the spring administration of the SAT

If your counselor believes that you performed well on the PSAT, then register for the spring SAT. Prepare for the SAT just as you did for the PSAT.

How to Prepare for the SAT

1. Ask your high school counselor for a copy of the SAT registration booklet. Study the sample test questions and answers it contains.
2. Go to your local bookstore or library and find a recent study guide to help you learn more about the types of questions on the test and how to answer them.
3. Buy a book with sample tests.
4. Create a weekly study schedule (5–6 hours) and stick to it.
5. Take as many sample tests as you can, and learn from your mistakes.

---

6. When preparing for this (or any other) standardized test, remember these tips:

- Find a comfortable pace—not too fast or too slow.
- Read each question carefully—know what is being asked.
- Don't "outsmart" the question—give the correct answer.
- Know the directions well—don't waste time reading them.
- Guessing isn't bad—eliminate answers and then guess from what is left.

What You'll Get Out of It

More than 98 percent of the four-year colleges in this country require that you submit scores from either the SAT or ACT examinations. Since most colleges take your highest SAT verbal and math score, there is no penalty for taking this test often. Starting your SAT testing experience in your sophomore year can help build your confidence and raise your score. Strong scores on the SAT, coupled with good grades in major courses, increase your chances of gaining admission to the colleges of your choice.

#14—Take the Spring Administration of the SAT II

Why Do It

Most students do not take any administration of the SAT II (formerly known as the Achievement Tests) until the end of their junior year or fall of their senior year, and then, only if they are applying to colleges that either recommend or require them.

You might want to consider taking one or more of the SAT II subject tests if:

- you are doing well in school (mostly A grades)

and

- you are taking an Honors, Accelerated, or Advanced Placement course in a subject that offers an SAT II subject test

How to Do It

First, talk to your high school counselor. If this professional believes that your academic performance to date and your course load warrants, register for the spring SAT II.

You should register for the June, not the early May, administration of the test. This extra month of class time is especially important because many teachers use this time to review the course. And that is the best type of preparation for the SAT II.

Once you have decided to take the SAT II, work with your counselor to select the subject(s) you should take. It is unlikely that you will be in more than one advanced-level course, so the choice should be fairly easy. When you register for this exam, note that it is unlike the other SAT exams. The SAT II is a one-hour exam that covers a particular subject, such as biology, chemistry, physics, writing, literature, history, mathematics, and foreign languages. If you have done well in a recent Honors, Accelerated, or Advanced Placement course, give the SAT II your best shot. You might be pleasantly surprised.

What You'll Get Out of It

Good grades in demanding courses are sure to impress college admission officers. Add in high scores on SAT II subject tests, and your chances of admission get even better!

#15—Tour College Campuses

Why Do It

The end of your sophomore year is a good time to reflect on your progress. Remember suggestion #9, which urged you to ask very specific questions of college graduates in order to learn more about their colleges? Do you also remember obtaining material from and about the colleges? Well, now is the time to visit some of those colleges. The visit is important for two reasons:

1. It will make the pages of printed material come alive for you.
2. It will demonstrate your sincere interest in a particular school to its admission office.

How to Do It

You never really get a sense of a college unless you take a good look around. Touring the campus is an excellent way to get a sense of the place.

Guidelines for a Successful College Visit

1. *Plan ahead.* Schedule your tour at least 7–14 days before your arrival.
2. *Give yourself time.* Don't rush, either from school to school, or when on campus. Allow yourself at least four hours on campus.
3. *Call to schedule your visit.* Speaking with another person when you schedule your visit is essential. Don't forget to ask the name of the person who is scheduling the visit. Otherwise, you have no way to check your arrangements or make any changes.
4. *Ask for confirmation.* Always request a written confirmation of your visit.
5. *Create a college journal.* For each college you visit, write down the specific reasons you're interested in this college (size, location, setting, academic programs, and any features you were impressed with in the brochures). This is your chance to check out each feature and record your observations about each school.

Remember, a campus tour is really a sales pitch that is scripted, packaged, and polished by the admission office. Here are your goals:

- Take a good look at what is shown to you (see the following list). Ask yourself whether the features you are shown are *really* important to you and whether this college has the features you want most.
- Scout for areas you would like to revisit after the "official" tour.

11 Things to Look For When You Take a Campus Tour

1. *Upkeep of the grounds.* The pride of a campus is reflected by the way a campus is kept.
2. *Condition of the buildings.* Take a look inside and out. Neglected buildings may indicate financial difficulties.
3. *New construction.* Generally speaking, new construction indicates financial stability and also shows the college's commitment to current and future students.
4. *Faculty offices.* The more time faculty members are available to work with students, the better. Look for regularly posted office hours, and for students and faculty talking together.
5. *Athletic and fitness facilities.* Note the condition of the facilities and the accessibility to the general student population.
6. *Residence halls and dormitories.* This may be your "home away from home," so note the:
    - general upkeep
    - security
    - various room arrangements (coed, freshmen only, etc.)
    - distance from classrooms
    - laundry, recreational, and study facilities
7. *Fraternities and sororities.* Inquire about their role on campus.
8. *Campus library.* Look for a blend of social atmosphere, technology, and books.
9. *Counseling and health facilities.* Knowing the range of treatment options is powerful information.
10. *Career Services/Graduate Placement Office.* Check out the activity and programs available to upper-class students.
11. *Dining halls.* Cleanliness, variety and cost of food, and optional meal plans are critical issues.

By checking out these things on the "official" tour, you will have gathered information to direct you on your own "unofficial" tour. Don't miss three wonderful sources of information:

- *Students.* Seek out a few and ask them questions.
- *Student newspaper.* It often presents a balanced picture of campus life and activities.
- *College personnel.* Ask questions of faculty, administrators, and others who work at the school. They are likely to give you a fairly balanced sense of the place.

The tour should help you decide whether you want to continue exploring the college, but did you know that your tour can also help you get into a college?

Colleges are interested in those students who are interested in them. They know that a student is more likely to accept their offer of admission if the student has been to the campus. Therefore, if the high school records are equal, colleges are impressed with, and more likely to accept, those students who have made the effort to visit the college and tour the campus.

What You'll Get Out of It

It's important to realize that the publications you receive from a college are designed to put the buildings, the campus, and the students in the best possible light. The only way to get the real picture is to visit the campus yourself.

The college visit also serves another important purpose. It shows the admission office that you are serious about the school, a fact that just might work in your favor should you decide to apply.

#16—Explore Summer High School Programs

Why Do It

Enrolling in a high school summer program can be a great way to prepare for college admission. You can take advantage of a summer program to:

- take "additional" courses you can't fit into your regular academic schedule
- enroll in courses that are "required for high school, but not essential for college"
- improve a less-than-outstanding grade
- obtain "extra help" in an academic area that is not your strength
- prepare for a very demanding course

How to Do It

Before making plans for the summer, check with two very important parties:

- your family
- your high school counselor

Your family might have plans of their own for you. They might want you to begin working on a job or to be available for a special family vacation, or they might be delighted that you want to consider a high school summer program.

Your counselor is essential because she or he knows:

- your academic record to date
- the high school course offerings
- your short- and long-term goals for college

In addition, your counselor has probably helped many students in the college exploration process. His or her knowledge can go a long way in helping you find the colleges that are the best "fits" for you.

By consulting both your family and your counselor, you can plan a summer that enables you to:

- enjoy a rest from school
- spend time with family and friends
- use the summer to address some academic issues

What You'll Get Out of It

College admission officers are impressed with happy and productive students. Knowing that you chose to devote extra time to your studies by enrolling in a summer program can make a favorable impression on admission officers.

junior year *in* high school

#17—Create Your Resume

Why Do It

By your junior year in high school, if you have worked through suggestions #1 to #16, you should have built a strong academic record and a long list of extracurricular activities. Now is the time to put these experiences to use by creating a resume. As you visit colleges in your junior and senior years of high school, this resume can help you present a complete picture of your accomplishments and interests.

Many colleges require that you provide an overview of your accomplishments and interests in your application for admission. If you have already set all this information down on paper, you have taken a giant step toward completing your college application. Your resume gives the reader a sense of:

- your accomplishments
- your interests in school (both in and out of the classroom)
- your interests outside school

How to Do It

Creating a resume may seem quite difficult, but it really is rather enjoyable. It is an opportunity for you to "put on paper" what you are all about.

There are many different formats for resumes. I suggest you emphasize three major aspects of your life:

- academic record
- extracurricular activities (both in and out of school)
- awards and honors

The example on page 54 shows one good way to present your resume.

What You'll Get Out of It

Resumes are important to college admission officers because they emphasize:

- organization
- accomplishment
- explanation

The sooner you become familiar with how to create and update your resume, the better you'll be able to present yourself to colleges at interviews and on your applications.

First, Middle, Last Name
Street Address
City, State, ZIP Code
Area Code and Telephone Number

Academic Record
- Name of High School, City, State (Years Attending)
- Grade Point Average on 4.0 Scale
- Listing of Accelerated, Honors, Advanced Placement Courses
- Standardized Testing Results (PSAT, SAT I and II, and ACT)

Extracurricular Activities
  School Activities
- Name of Activity, Number of Years Involved
    (explanation of activity and your role)
    (Example: School Newspaper - *Golden Cougar* - 2 years
        Writer - wrote and submitted articles for publication - 9th grade
        Advertising Manager - solicited ads for newspaper - 10th grade)
- Name of Activity, Number of Years Involved
    (explanation of activity and your role)
    (Example: Student Government - 2 years
        Class Representative - represented class in Student Senate - 9th grade
        Student Body Treasurer - balanced student body fund - 10th grade)

  Community Activities
- Name of Activity, Number of Years Involved
    (explanation of activity and your role)
    (Example: Lector at Mass - St. Mary's of the Lake - monthly - 9th and
        10th grades, gave readings at Saturday evening masses)
- Name of Activity, Number of Years Involved
    (explanation of activity and your role)
    (Example: Aide to Nurse's Aide at Millers Manor - weekly - 9th and
        10 grades, helped entertain nursing home patients)

Awards or Honors
- Name of Award or Honor, When Awarded
    (explanation of award or honor)
    (Example: National Honor Society - awarded in May of 10th grade,
        awarded to top 5% of students at conclusion of sophomore year)

#18—Attend College Presentations at Your High School

Why Do It

Throughout the year, high schools host college admission representatives. During their visits to high school, these individuals:

- give brief (20–30 minute) presentations
- answer questions of students
- schedule afternoon or evening interviews with students and families

These representatives are "decision makers." They play a major role in determining who will or will not gain admission to their colleges. As a prospective applicant, you should make time to meet with all the representatives who come to your school.

How to Do It

Taking time out of your academic schedule to visit college representatives can be tricky. On the one hand, you need to be in class to earn good grades. On the other hand, learning more about a particular college might help you narrow your list of possibilities, and making a connection with the representative might give your college application some special attention.

Before planning to miss class, meet with your college advisor to learn:

- how to get permission from the teacher to miss the class
- what you can do to make up the work you miss
- the time, date, and location of the college representative's visit to your school
- the length of time the representative will be visiting your school
- the possibility of visiting with the representative for a few minutes before or after the presentation to discuss your resume and share your interest in the college

The important message you need to communicate is that you:

- have done your homework on the college
- have questions you would like to discuss
- have serious interest in the college

What You'll Get Out of It

Setting yourself apart from other candidates for admission is one way to receive special attention that may help you gain admission to your top-choice colleges. Obtaining more information about colleges from the admission representatives who visit your school and making sure they remember you in a positive way are important objectives. Being prepared with your resume and some excellent questions about the school sets you apart from the many students the representative sees throughout the day.

#19—Go to Local College Fairs

Why Do It

A college fair is nothing more than dozens of college representatives each sitting behind a table piled high with information about his or her school. Because a large number of schools are represented in one convenient place, a college fair offers a great opportunity for students and their parents to learn a lot about many different schools.

How to Do It

College fairs are an opportunity to make another contact with someone from your prime college list. Remember, it never hurts to have two admission officers (decision makers) on your side when your application is reviewed.

10 Ways to Get the Most Out of Any College Fair

1. Obtain a list of the colleges represented.
2. Contact the admission offices at those colleges on your prime list and ask the name of the representative attending the fair.
3. Make a list of any questions or issues you would like to discuss.
4. Ask your high school counselor the best times to visit the fair. (Try to avoid those times that are very crowded.)
5. Time your meeting with the college representative so that few people are around.
6. Bring your resume and transcript to share.
7. Express all that you have done to date to exhibit your interest in the college (meeting the representative at your high school and touring the campus last spring or summer).
8. Inform the representative that you would like to visit the campus in the summer or fall for an interview and want to know the best time.
9. Ask the representative for a business card.
10. Write a follow-up "nice to meet you at the college fair . . . hope to see you on campus soon" note.

What You'll Get Out of It

Those students who explore their options thoroughly always seem to gain admission to their top-choice college. If you think about it, it makes sense. After all, they are stacking the deck in their favor by doing everything they can to learn about colleges and to make their interests known to the schools they are considering.

Although attending a college fair may not seem that critical to some, it is another point of contact with an admission office representative. These contacts add up and, combined with a strong record, could make the difference between being admitted or rejected at the colleges of your choice.

#20—Get to Know Your College Advisor

Why Do It

Up to this point in the book, I have emphasized the value of working with your high school counselor. Now it's time to meet with your college advisor.

At most schools, the college advisor has two important functions:

1. Guiding you through the maze of the college exploration, application, and selection process
2. Writing your counselor recommendation to each of the colleges

In short, this person plays a very important role in your future. You certainly should put a great deal of effort into getting to know your college advisor.

How to Do It

The best way to get to know your college advisor is to schedule an appointment with him or her. You may want to consider inviting your parents to join in this meeting.

When you meet with your college advisor, you (not your parents) should do the following:

1. Present and explain in detail your updated resume.
2. Discuss the criteria that you have determined are a good "starting point" for your initial college explorations.
3. Share your impressions of the colleges you have toured to date.
4. Ask whether the advisor can suggest other colleges that might possibly be good "fits" for you.
5. Ask for specific details about your advisor's:
   - process of college exploration
   - application timetable
   - role in representing you to the colleges through recommendation and/or telephone calls to the colleges in your behalf

When you leave this meeting, you and your parents should have a fairly strong sense of whether your advisor is going to:

- guide you throughout the process
- suggest additional colleges for you to explore
- represent you to the colleges in a "proactive" manner

It's a good idea to ask your advisor whether there is written material that outlines his or her services. If the answer is yes, and you are impressed with the person, rejoice! If you are not so pleased, read on, for other assistance may be available. Whatever you do, try not to offend the college advisor. After all, he or she will be the author of the recommendation that will accompany your application to each college.

What You'll Get Out of It

The college advisor is an important person in your college plans. The resources, knowledge, "contacts" with admission office colleagues, and responsibility for providing the school recommendation give this individual the opportunity to play a pivotal role in your admission options.

The ideal relationship is one in which you and your advisor consult, discuss, and ponder the "fit" between you and the colleges that interest you and whether the advisor represents you to each college in a proactive and positive manner.

#21—Take the SAT in Fall and Spring

Why Do It

When evaluating candidates for admission, colleges place the highest degree of importance on the courses you have taken and the grades you have received. In many cases, the next most important criteria are your scores on standardized college entrance tests. Among the most widely accepted examinations is the Scholastic Assessment Test (SAT).

Because this test is very important in the college admission process, I strongly recommend that you plan to take the SAT in both the fall and the spring. Most colleges care only about the highest combined score, so it rarely hurts your chances for admission if you take the test multiple times. The one exception to this rule is that, after repeated attempts, your scores actually remain the same or decrease.

How to Do It

Start by discussing the SAT with your college advisor. He or she can assist by doing the following:

1. Guide you through the registration booklet.
2. Advise you to take both the fall *and* spring administrations of the test to make sure you get the highest possible score.
3. Share any "hints or tips" about taking these or any other standardized tests (see suggestion #8).
4. Review with you your PSAT results to locate strengths or weaknesses.
5. Build your confidence so that you can do your best on the examinations.
6. Discuss your test results with you and your family and help you prepare for the next round of examinations.

The bottom line is this: Generally speaking, the more you take these examinations, the more familiar you are with them, the more confident you become—and the higher your scores!

What You'll Get Out of It

On the one hand, given that the results of these examinations are important to most colleges, it makes sense to take them seriously. On the other hand, these results are only one piece of the college admission puzzle. The best advice is to view your application as a whole, and these exams as an important part of the whole.

When it comes to the SAT, the best course is to give it your best shot early and often, to review the results carefully, and to go for it again if necessary.

#22—Consider an Independent College Advisor

Why Do It

Your college advisor can be an important part of your college exploration, application, and selection process. Even though your high school has a college advisor, you and your family may prefer to work with an independent college advisor. These individuals have no ties with any high school. Rather, they have their own private practices in which they assist students throughout the application process.

Students and their families may turn to an independent college advisor when they:

- are convinced the high school college advisor is too busy for them
- are unsure of the ability or knowledge of their college advisor
- want a second opinion to support or confirm that of the high school college advisor
- desperately need guidance from someone not related to their high school

How to Do It

The best way to identify qualified independent counselors is through their association. You can request a list of counselors by writing to the following association:

Independent Educational Counselors Association
4805 Chain Bridge Road, Suite 401
Fairfax, VA 22030

When the complete list of names, addresses, and services arrives, use this three-step approach to make your choice.

How to Choose an Independent College Advisor

1. Locate those independent counselors within a reasonable distance of your home.
2. Contact these counselors and inquire about:

- specific services (surveys to students *and* parents, testing, and specific contact with colleges)
- hours
- fee and payment scale

3. Meet with each counselor in his or her office and inquire about:
   - degrees
   - references (both former clients and college admission personnel)
   - names of colleges visited in the last year
   - related job experiences

Be thorough and check out all the references. Be cautious in believing any claims or guarantees. Ask as many questions as you like. Always trust your "gut" reactions. Discuss the decision as a family and don't allow yourself to be forced into working with someone you don't like.

What You'll Get Out of It

Independent counselors can bring a great deal of expertise to the college exploration, application, and selection process. Their wealth of unique and special experiences can provide insight not typically found in most high school counselors.

While independent counselors are not for every student, some students and families have turned to these individuals with a great deal of success.

#23—Get to Know Your Junior Year Teachers

Why Do It

Colleges are most interested in learning about the academic abilities of their applicants. Where do they get this information? Straight from your high school teachers.

In order to learn about your strength as a student, many colleges ask applicants for recommendations from their teachers. The comments made by teachers are reviewed very carefully by college admission officers.

Therefore, it is wise to select those teachers who can discuss in detail your ability to contribute to the classroom. In deciding which teachers to select, consider carefully those instructors who have worked with you most recently and over the longest period of time. Generally speaking, these would be your junior year teachers.

How to Do It

Start with the source—the actual recommendation forms. Read them carefully, and they will guide you in your selection. Typically, they recommend:

- teachers of a major subject (English, foreign language, math, science, or social studies)
- teachers who have worked with you recently (junior year) and extensively (a year or more)
- teachers with whom you have done good work (minimum of a B grade)

Once you have selected those teachers who meet the colleges' criteria, it's time for you to make a special effort to get to know these instructors. Make an appointment with the teacher to discuss your:

- performance in class—specifically ask how you can improve
- college and career goals—feel comfortable enough to share your resume
- activities both in and out of school
- hopes and dreams for the future

By doing this, you gain a clear sense of which junior year teachers you can approach in the fall of your senior year to write your teacher recommendations.

What You'll Get Out of It

Most admission professionals look to teacher recommendations for an insight into your ability to handle college-level work. A recommendation from a teacher who knows you well and can comment knowledgeably about your classroom work can help your chances of acceptance. However, a recommendation that consists of merely vague general statements about your grades will do little to further your cause and may be viewed as a lost opportunity.

If you are careful in your selection of the teachers you ask to write your recommendations, and if you give them a good sense of your educational goals, you can increase your chances of getting into your first-choice colleges.

#24—Take the Junior Spring ACT

Why Do It

You already know that standardized tests are an important factor in college admission decisions. In short, since courses and grades vary so much from school to school, these examinations are the one constant that colleges can use to compare applicants.

Whatever your opinion of standardized tests, until or unless someone convinces all colleges that these examinations are meaningless, it is wise to place value in them. With this in mind, in addition to taking the SAT in both the fall and spring of your junior year (suggestion #21), you should also consider taking the ACT in the spring of your junior year.

Each year, more and more colleges are accepting either the SAT or the ACT to satisfy the standardized testing requirement. You can "hedge your bets" by taking both exams during your junior year.

How to Do It

As with the PSAT and the SAT, your college advisor can help you by doing the following:

1. Guide you through the registration booklet.
2. Share any "hints or tips" about taking these or any standardized tests (see suggestion #8).
3. Build your confidence so that you can do your best on the examinations.
4. Discuss your test results with you and your family and help you prepare for the next round of examinations.

What You'll Get Out of It

Most colleges care about the results of the standardized tests. This is especially true about almost all of the "selective" colleges.

By taking these exams "early and often," you are increasing the probability of boosting your scores. It is critical to recognize that strong grades, difficult courses, and good test scores are a nearly unbeatable combination when it comes to gaining admission to the college of your choice.

#25—Arrange for a Campus Interview or Group Session

Why Do It

At first glance, you may be wondering why making arrangements for a campus interview or group session is important to gaining admission. The answer is simple: Most students and their families do not take advantage of this wonderful opportunity.

On the one hand, these sessions are important because they are an opportunity for you to learn a great deal about each college you visit. On the other hand, these sessions can be viewed by admission officers as a serious expression of your interest in the college. In some cases, this display of interest may make the difference between being accepted or rejected by a college.

How to Do It

When scheduling a campus interview or group session, you should follow these guidelines.

Scheduling an Interview

1. Plan ahead—a minimum of two to three weeks is reasonable.
2. Budget your time—allow at least four hours for your visit.
3. Ask for the name of the person scheduling the appointment—just in case.
4. Request a written confirmation. It clarifies your appointment.
5. Have a date and time in mind; weekdays are best, but be flexible.
6. Request that the interview or group session be first, and the tour later. It's good to be fresh at the interview.
7. Request a meeting with others. Consider financial aid officers, faculty, coaches.
8. Choose a personal interview over a group session. It's more personal.
9. Bring materials, such as your resume or high school transcript.

What You'll Get Out of It

When it comes to campus interviews, a little advance planning can have a lot of positive results. To begin with, you allow yourself and your family to get an up-close-and-personal view of the college. In addition, you are taking advantage of this opportunity to leave a very positive impression of yourself. All things being equal (and they sometimes are), the student who makes the proper arrangements should have a great visit that will lead to the opportunity to spend the next four years at the college.

#26—Make Your Interview Count

Why Do It

Many students are intimidated by the campus interview. Try to look at your interview as a conversation or an exchange of information and impressions.

When you think about it, both you and the college interviewer have four common goals:

1. You both want to "sell" something. The interviewer is pushing the college, and you are pushing yourself.
2. You both have questions.
3. You both have answers.
4. You both want to make a positive impression on the other.

How to Do It

There are certain things you can do to make your interview a very positive experience.

---

11 Steps to a Successful Interview

1. *Do your homework.* Thoroughly research the college before arrival.
2. *Arrive early.* With 15 to 20 minutes to spare before the scheduled interview, you'll feel less rushed and more comfortable.
3. *Greet the interviewer with a firm handshake.* It expresses confidence.
4. *Introduce those who are with you.* It's polite and puts everyone at ease.
5. *Bring materials with you.* Come with questions, a resume, and your transcript.
6. *Get comfortable.* Relax and be prepared to listen and share.
7. *Enjoy yourself.* You are the center of attention; enjoy it.
8. *Speak directly to the interviewer.* Making eye contact is important.
9. *Open your mouth and talk.* It's time to share.
10. *Don't forget to breathe.* This is not a race; relax and enjoy the conversation.
11. *Be yourself.* The interviewer is not looking for anything other than you.

You are likely to be asked three questions in any interview. Knowing these questions in advance allows you to prepare for them. Here are the top three interview questions:

1. Why are you here?
2. What's your story?
3. What questions can I answer for you?

Let's look at each of these questions and consider how best to prepare your answer. Remember, these responses are only suggestions. Your
comments should be your own.

Question One: Why are you here?

Be direct and specific when answering why you are exploring a particular college. Here are some suggested answers:

1. "I'm looking at colleges that have certain features that are important to me, such as (insert features such as size, location, setting,
   and academic program)."

   These specific features will only reinforce the opinion of the
   interviewer that your reasons are logical.

2. "I've reviewed your material, and I'm impressed with certain
   features/programs like (share those features/programs that
   impressed you from the information)."

   This answer indicates that you have done your homework by
   thoroughly reviewing the material from the college.

3. "I was referred here by a counselor/friend/family member who
   knows me well and thinks this college might be a great match."

   This answer indicates you have explored much more than just
   written material from the college.

Question Two: What's your story?

Most people find it difficult to talk about themselves. You may be shy, or
perhaps you don't know where to begin. In any event, try to break your
"story" into three areas:

1. Talk about yourself as a student. Be prepared for a follow-up question. Share information such as:
   - grade point average (GPA)
   - rank in class
   - honors or accelerated courses
   - standardized test (SAT or ACT) results
2. Talk about yourself outside the classroom. Share information such as:
   - clubs to which you belong (both school and community)
   - sports in which you participate
   - hobbies

3. Talk about yourself as a person. Share information about:

- goals for the future
- career interests (including any jobs held)
- family and friends

Question Three: What questions can I answer for you?

This question—and your response—are very important. Under no circumstances should you say, "None." This is your opportunity to obtain specific information or address any concerns. It is also an excellent chance to show not only what you know about the college, but also that you have specific questions about this college.

The key to this question is to thoroughly review the material from the college, create a list of questions, and be prepared to ask them during the interview. Again, the questions listed below are only suggestions. Ask only questions you care about. Some examples of the types of questions you might want to ask include:

1. I've been looking at (names of a few colleges that are similar to the one you are visiting). What features do you feel distinguish this college from them?

2. What specific changes are planned for this college in the next two, five, ten years?

3. I've reviewed your material and think the advising system looks interesting. How likely is it that I will be assigned an academic advisor in my prospective major during my freshman year?

4. Based on my resume and high school transcript, how competitive an applicant am I for this college?

One more suggestion can make your visit complete. When you return home, take a few minutes to write a thank-you letter to your interviewer. It's a nice touch, it shows class, and it will probably end up in your application file.

What You'll Get Out of It

A positive interview can make a significant impact in the college admission process. Some admission officers claim the interview is only informational and has no evaluative role, yet many admission professionals say that students who do well on their interviews greatly enhance their chances of admission.

At the very least, the interview can help you judge the "fit" between you and the college. However, why not take any opportunity to increase your chances for admission by preparing correctly for this exchange. It might just make the difference in your plans for the next four years.

#27—Make a Positive Impression in a Group Session

Why Do It

The group session is a meeting that takes place either before or after the campus tour. Several prospective applicants and their families are greeted by a member of the admission office staff, and over the next 30–60 minutes are typically:

- shown a brief video presentation on the college
- given a brief sales pitch
- asked if they have any questions
- thanked for visiting the college and then dismissed

Unlike the personal interviews, group sessions are not designed for you to make much of an individual impression. However, there are things you can do to make a positive impression on the admission office decision makers both during and after the session.

How to Do It

Although there is little opportunity to make any sort of impression during the video presentation or the sales pitch, there are some things you can do to be noticed in a positive way during the group session. In fact, since most students do not explore this opportunity, you will have very little competition.

7 Things You Can Do to Make a Positive Impression in the Group Session

1. *Dress in the same manner you would for the personal interview.* Wear neat and comfortable clothes.
2. *Carefully review material from and about the college.* Bring good questions.
3. *Sit near the front of the room.* You want to be clearly seen.
4. *Write down the name and title of the admission representative giving the presentation.* You will soon be writing to this individual.
5. *Ask the questions you have prepared during the question-and-answer period.* Don't be shy, but be polite.

6. *At the conclusion of the session, approach the presenter, introduce yourself, and ask a couple of good follow-up questions.* You may want to present a copy of your transcript and resume for review.
7. *Within 3–5 days of the presentation, send a thank-you note and offer to keep in touch.* Then do so regularly.

What You'll Get Out of It

So much of the admission process is viewed as a competition—one student against another. Rarely is there an opportunity to stand apart from other prospective applicants. By using this seven-step approach, you distinguish yourself from other possible applicants, and as a result, you may give yourself an edge in gaining admission to the college of your choice.

#28—Attend "Open House" Events

Why Do It

One of the most ignored activities sponsored by admission offices is the "Open House" event. Perhaps families feel they won't get much individual attention at such large functions. But, in fact, open houses can serve as an excellent introduction to a school. Usually videos are shown, tours are offered, the campus is "spruced up," and those closest to the college can "show off" the many faces of the institution.

How to Do It

You want to do more than just attend an open house. You want to actually meet some of the admission office decision makers.

Making the Most of an Open House

1. Arrive a bit early.
2. Check in with the admission office.
3. Ask for the name of the admission officer responsible for your geographic area or letter of the alphabet.
4. Locate that admission officer.
5. Schedule a few minutes to "chat."
6. Present your resume and transcript.
7. Treat your conversation like an interview (see suggestion #26).

It is highly unlikely that this admission officer will be approached in this manner by other applicants. Most students and their families miss out on this excellent opportunity to establish a personal contact with the admission professionals who will review their applications.

What You'll Get Out of It

An open house is a wonderful opportunity for a fairly shy person to get a detailed sense of the college. By being proactive with this campus event, you encourage an admission professional to take a closer look at your academic record and to explore your desire to attend the college. This aggressive approach to college admission may just result in an offer of admission.

#29—Meet with College Faculty When Visiting Colleges

Why Do It

Faculty members are some of the most influential people on college campuses. In addition to teaching classes, conducting research, and taking an active role in governance, they work closely with students as advisors and mentors.

Students visiting campus rarely ask to meet with faculty. Perhaps they view faculty members as too busy or too far removed from the admission process. Indeed, faculty members are always busy, but at many colleges they do play a role in admission. Getting to know a faculty member can help your cause—especially if you make a favorable impression that results in a personal recommendation to the admission office.

With this in mind, I strongly suggest that you include a visit with a member of the faculty on your agenda when visiting colleges. This person may be a great asset to your admission efforts.

How to Do It

When arranging your visit to each college, try to set up a meeting with a faculty member. Here's what you should do:

- Ask to meet with a faculty member in an area of particular interest to you.
- Prepare for your meeting in the same manner as you would the interview (see suggestion #26). Being prepared is *always a* good idea.
- Ask some specific questions that interest you, such as:

  How would you describe the level of student and faculty interaction at this college?

  What is the average number of hours per week that faculty are available for office hours?

  Are students involved in the evaluation of faculty performance in the classroom?

  From your perception as a faculty member, what are the three best things about this college, and what three things would you quickly change?

- Write a "thank you for meeting with me" note when you return home.

It might be wise to keep in contact with this person to let him or her know how you are doing and to discuss your application plans to the college.

What You'll Get Out of It

One can never be sure about the impact of certain people in the admission process. However, the opportunity to get a faculty member's perspective on a college is valuable in itself. In addition, a note or call to the admission office from this person might just make a difference in your admission to the college of your choice.

#30—Attend a Summer Program at Your "Top Choice" College

Why Do It

Many students view attending any type of a summer program as a punishment. In fact, nothing could be further from the truth.

Attending a summer program at a college you truly care about can give you a real sense of the place (albeit a "summer" sense), and may afford you a chance to meet people who can make a difference in your application to the college.

How to Do It

Early in the summer program, you might want to consider looking carefully for:

- a friendly admission officer
- a professor who works at the college year-round
- a professor who doesn't work there year-round

These three types of individuals can all assist you if:

- they get to know you
- they believe you will contribute to the college community
- they are convinced you can and will do fine academic work

My suggestion is that you approach any of these individuals and ask them very specific questions about yourself. If they do not know your ability, shine in the classroom, and they will take notice. The instructors will not only provide comments and feedback, but many would be happy to write a recommendation to this or any other college you are considering.

What You'll Get Out of It

You have learned a bit about finding the "edge" in the college admission process. While you may think some of these suggestions are unnecessary, many candidates are willing to explore every option to get into college. Any "edge" you can find is a good one if it helps you gain admission to the college of your choice.

#31—Contact a Trustee in Your Area

Why Do It

In over 18 years of experience, I have worked at a wide variety of educational institutions. At each college, I have been asked to take a close look at a particular file by Board of Trustee members. In essence, their unspoken message was very clear. They wanted the student represented in the file to gain admission to the institution.

There is no reason to hide this opportunity from you. However, if you choose to use it, here are some things you should know:

- Reserve this tactic for your top-choice college only.
- Realize that it can take a lot of time and effort to reach the trustee.
- Be prepared to represent yourself in a very thorough manner.

How to Do It

Once you have decided which college is your top choice, follow these guidelines:

1. Review the course catalog or curriculum guide to locate the names of the current Board of Trustees.
2. Find out the city and state where each Board member resides.
3. Identify the Board member nearest you.
4. Use directory assistance or the white pages of the telephone book to find the address and phone number of this trustee.
5. Decide whether you want to call or write to the trustee.
6. If you decide to telephone, review your material from the college and be prepared to explain clearly, concisely, and compellingly:
   - why you are interested in this college
   - how you learned about it
   - why you should gain admission
   - what you feel you can offer the college
7. If you decide to write, make these same four points the focus of your letter and be sure to include:
   - your resume
   - your latest transcript
   - a complete listing of your standardized test results
8. In either event, ask the trustee for a face-to-face meeting to discuss the college further.

9. If the trustee agrees to meet, treat this meeting as you would an interview (see suggestion #26).

10. After the meeting, write a thank-you note that:
    - thanks the trustee for his or her time
    - states that you would appreciate anything the trustee could do on your behalf with the admission office to help you gain admission to this school

11. If the trustee does not want to meet, simply ask whether you can keep in touch about developments in school.

What You'll Get Out of It

People serving on any college Board of Trustees are very proud of the particular college.

Although they may hear about admission procedures, they usually have little or no contact with that office.

By contacting a trustee, you are indicating your serious interest in the college. That alone gives you and the trustee something in common—and makes it unlikely that the trustee will ignore you.

In any event, a call, letter, or fax from a trustee to the admission office makes people sit up and take notice. It might be just what you need to move the admission officers to see what a wonderful asset you would be to their school.

#32—Take Advanced Placement (AP) Examinations

Why Do It

Always take the Advanced Placement exam whenever you complete an advanced placement or honors course. That's when the material is fresh in your mind, and that's when you are most likely to perform well. It is a mistake to wait until your senior year to take a test based on a course you completed in your sophomore or junior year.

How to Do It

Before taking an Advanced Placement (AP) course, you should ask the teacher whether the culmination of this course is to take the test. If your instructor answers yes, you are all set. If the instructor answers no, see your college advisor for advice.

If the teacher says that the exam will be administered, it would be wise to inquire about the following issues:

1. How best to study for the exam
   - Your need for additional materials for preparation
   - How much time you should allow for preparation
   - Whether you should prepare through group study
2. How the course best prepares you for the test
   - What areas you should focus on

Remember the following six-step plan to help you prepare for any AP exam.

Preparing for AP Exams

1. Ask your teacher or high school counselor for a copy of the AP registration booklet, which contains sample test questions and answers.
2. Go to your local bookstore or library and find a recent study guide to help you learn the types of questions that appear on the test—and how you should answer them.
3. Buy a book with sample tests.
4. Create a weekly study schedule (5–6 hours) and stick to it.
5. Take as many sample tests as you can, and learn from your mistakes.

6. Learn the tricks smart test-takers know:
- Find a comfortable pace—not too fast or too slow.
- Read each question carefully—know what it is asking.
- Don't "outsmart" the question—give the correct answer.
- Know the directions well—don't waste time reading them.
- Guessing isn't bad—eliminate answers and then guess from what is left.

What You'll Get Out of It

Colleges care about students who take a demanding course load in high school. These are the students who are most likely to succeed in college as well.

Some colleges use AP scores only for placement into college courses after a student is admitted. In these cases, the scores do not have much impact on admission. Other schools, however, regard AP courses as excellent preparation for college and look favorably on applicants who do well on AP tests.

By taking both the course and the exam, you may demonstrate to college admission representatives that you are well prepared to gain admission to their college.

senior
year *in* high school

#33—Enroll in Courses at Your Local College

Why Do It

In general, college courses are more demanding than high school courses. With this in mind, it might be wise to explore the possibility of taking a course or two at your local college. It is not necessary that this college be one that you are considering attending. Enrolling in a college-level course and doing well is a good sign that you are ready for college work.

How to Do It

As with many ideas focused on college admission, I suggest you start by meeting with your college advisor. This might be an excellent time to ask specific questions about the following:

- *Your course load.* Is it full enough, or should you consider taking a course at your local college as well?
- *The experience of your counselor in this area.* Have other students done this before? If yes, with what outcome?
- *The nature of the courses.* Is the credit you receive from the course transferable to all colleges?
- *Additional issues.* Is there someone your counselor might recommend you speak with at the college for additional information?

After talking with your counselor, meet with a representative from the college to discuss the following:

- Admission policy of the college for high school students
- Cost of taking the course and available financial aid if desired
- Experience of transferring courses taken by high school students to other colleges

What You'll Get Out of It

You learned early in this book that one of the most impressive things admission representatives could find in an application was good grades in demanding courses. Obviously, these same representatives would also be impressed with good grades in college courses. Both examples are clear indications that the candidate for admission can do well in the college classroom.

#34—Consider the "Early Action" and "Early Decision" Options

Why Do It

One of the biggest changes in the college admission process in the last few years is the option for students to express their interest in a particular college and learn of the college's decision "early" in the process. Two particular opportunities selected by students are "Early Action" and "Early Decision." These application options are available at only a few colleges, usually the most competitive in the field.

Under the Early Action plan, you apply by a particular date, usually in the early fall, and receive the admission decision as soon as possible afterward. If admitted, you can enroll immediately, or you can wait until May 1, the National Candidate's Reply Date, to decide.

Early Action

Advantages

- The applicant pool is smaller than for a "Regular" decision.
- You get your answer early in the process.
- If admitted, you are under less academic pressure.
- You are not required to attend.

Disadvantages

- The pool consists of *very* talented applicants.
- You run the risk of not gaining admission.
- If your application is deferred, it may be viewed as flawed.

Under the Early Decision option, you also apply by a particular date and receive the decision soon afterward. However, unlike Early Action, once you are admitted under Early Decision, you are obligated to withdraw any other applications, not submit future applications, and enroll at that college.

Early Decision

Advantages

- You have a way to express your serious interest in your first-choice colleges.
- If admitted, you are under less pressure.
- The applicant pool is smaller than for a "Regular" decision.
- If applying for financial aid, you run no risk of the college's resources being exhausted.

Disadvantages

- The pool consists of *very* talented applicants.
- If admitted, you must attend—you cannot reconsider later.
- If deferred, your application may be viewed as flawed.
- If applying for financial aid, you have much less negotiation room.

How to Do It

At first glance, these "Early" options may seem like great ideas. If available at the colleges you are considering, "Early" may be an excellent way for you to apply.

Before deciding on "Early" anything, it's a good idea to arrange a meeting with your college advisor and your parents to discuss the following issues:

1. If considering Early Decision, am I really committed to attend that one college? Is it really my first choice? Have I explored all other options carefully? It is always amazing to me how many students decide to apply Early Decision without ever having visited the college.

2. Based on my courses, grades, and scores, what are my chances for admission? Am I showing the colleges my best in terms of courses, grades, and scores, or do I have a weakness or two that I should work on, applying for Regular admission at a later date? Do my chances improve or decrease because I am considering Early Decision? It might be helpful for your college advisor to contact the particular college in question, fax your resume and transcript to the admission office, and gain valuable guidance from those admission officers who will evaluate your application. This is the procedure we follow at The Culver Academies.

3. What are the financial aid issues involved in Early Decision? It is true that Early Decision candidates are among the first to receive aid that year, but what if the financial aid offer is not enough and/or nonnegotiable? Read the Early Decision Contract carefully to see if you have an "out" if you and the college are unable to agree on financial aid resources available.

The key to making this decision is asking yourself two questions: Is this really the college I want to attend, and if so, is this the best way to apply? You may need others (parents, college advisor, admission representatives, etc.) to help you answer these questions, but they must be asked.

What You'll Get Out of It

If you decide to apply either Early Action or Early Decision, you do so with the understanding that you have:

- thoroughly explored the options and weighed the "pros and cons"
- received counsel from people who care about you
- reached a decision based on facts, statistics, and what you feel is best for you

You should take a moment to give yourself a pat on the back. This formula is a great way to make any big decision. Hopefully, you can build on this lesson over the next four years as you attend the college of your choice.

#35—Apply to a Range of Colleges

Why Do It

Applying to college is not a science. In other words, it is not an activity with a predictable result. With so many factors at work in each application (quality of courses, grades, score results, extracurricular activities, etc.), it is almost impossible to predict the results of all admission decisions.

In an effort to be "safe rather than sorry," most high school counselors have developed a "range" in which we ask that students place their college applications. I subscribe to the following range:

- "Reach"—chance of admission is less than 50 percent
- "Ballpark"—chance of admission is 50 percent
- "Looks Good"—chance of admission is greater than 50 percent

How to Do It

Placing the colleges to which you have decided to submit applications in this "range" is best done with the help of your college advisor.

Here are the questions you should ask:

1. Based on my courses, grades, and scores, in which of the three categories does each college on my list fall?

   Listen very carefully to the advice provided. You may be either frustrated or overjoyed by what your advisor says; but if you have confidence in your college advisor, you should trust his or her advice.

2. To how many colleges should I submit applications?

   Although there is no definitive answer, I have always been most comfortable recommending that students apply to two colleges per category. I say this for the following reasons:

   - While "Reaches" are less likely to admit you, you never know unless you give it your best try. It is fine to hope, but do not expect to gain admission to theses colleges. If you do not gain admission to a "Reach" school, you should realize that the decision is not so much a "rejection" of you and your high school record, but rather an acknowledgment that stronger applicants were offered admission for a limited number of spaces. That may not make you feel better right away, but it will later.

- The "Ballpark" category will likely provide you with a balance of offers—that is, schools you are most excited about that offer you admission. You might want to consider having more colleges in this category.
- Even though the "Looks Good" category might contain the colleges you are least excited about, you should be able to say that you would gladly attend any college in this category if the others don't offer you admission. Frankly, if you follow all the advice in this book, you may not even need these colleges.

What You'll Get Out of It
The goal of this book is to help you gain admission to the colleges of your choice. If you work with your college advisor to make sure that you are applying to colleges that span a range of realistic options, it is very likely that you will enroll at an institution that excites you and will help you get a good start on your future.

#36—Become Aware of College Relationships with Your High School

Why Do It

In any given year, students graduating from high school attend a wide variety of colleges. Last year, at The Culver Academies, my 151 seniors enrolled in 87 different colleges. I view this diversity of colleges as a very positive thing in that I encourage our students to explore a wide range of colleges.

Many college advisors work closely with college admission representatives. The admission representatives may visit particular high schools annually or semiannually, and a sense of familiarity may be established between certain colleges and particular high schools. These colleges come to know the quality of certain high schools' academic programs and may feel very comfortable with a wide range of applicants from these high schools. Because graduates from these high schools perform well at these colleges, admission representatives are more likely to admit a wider variety of students from these high schools.

How to Do It

Before finalizing the list of colleges to which you will apply, meet with your college advisor and ask:

1. Are there colleges with which your high school has a particularly good relationship that should be added to your list?
2. Are there particular colleges that have a history of not enrolling students from your high school because of their unfamiliarity with your school?
3. Are there colleges on your list that are more difficult to get into because of a "negative" relationship between your high school and a particular college?

There is little doubt that it is not fair for you to be viewed more or less favorably because of a relationship between a particular college and your high school, but the reality is that such factors may affect the way in which your application is viewed.

With good advice from your counselor, you might be able to take positive advantage of any relationships that exist between your high school and a particular college. Remember, information is power. It is to your advantage to be informed.

What You'll Get Out of It

Recognizing that relationships, both positive and negative, may exist between your high school and particular colleges is important information you can use to your benefit in the college admission process. This knowledge will help guide you toward or away from certain colleges.

#37—Submit a Graded Writing Sample

Why Do It

As you reflect on all the academic material included in your applications (courses, grades, and standardized test scores), you might notice a particular area of "weakness" in your record. Perhaps it might be:

- lower grades in humanities or social science courses
- a low score in the verbal section of your SAT
- a low score in the English section of the ACT

Instead of hoping that colleges won't notice these weaknesses, you can address them "head on" by submitting a graded paper or writing sample of which you are especially proud.

Taking this proactive approach sends a very clear message to the colleges. It says four things:

1. You are not trying to hide something—acknowledging a less than stellar performance in the past is another way of being honest.
2. You are addressing the weakness—sending a graded paper or writing sample is a way of saying that you will not simply be judged by one grade or score.
3. You are proving that you can do better work—the paper or writing sample is an excellent way of offering an alternative exhibit or substitute example of your ability to do college-level work.
4. You are doing better work—while submitting a paper or writing sample is fine, correcting the "weakness" with better grades or higher scores is what the colleges are expecting.

How to Do It

If, after reflecting on your record, you find a particular weakness you would like to address, you might want to meet with a few of your teachers to discuss your work. Ask them to consider your past papers or writing samples to help you choose one that can help make your case. The sample you choose should have these characteristics:

- *Reasonable length.* Admission representatives are more likely to read a paper or writing sample that is 2–5 pages than one that is 10–20 pages.

- *A grade of B or higher.* While it isn't necessary that the grade be an A, it would be foolish to send a paper with a grade lower than a B.
- *Extensive teacher comments.* For most admission representatives, the comments provided by the teacher are the key to the paper.

Once you have selected a sample that meets these criteria, send it off to the admission office with a note like this:

Dear Admission Committee:

In reviewing my academic record, you might be concerned about my (verbal test scores/humanities or social science grades). I have enclosed this paper (writing sample) to provide a clear example of my ability to do the level of work expected at (name of college).

Please view this material as part of my application. Thank you for your consideration.

Sincerely,
(your name and social security number)

What You'll Get Out of It

There's no doubt about it. College representatives *do* notice things like bad grades in a particular subject or low test scores. They are also interested in learning whether the student has addressed this area of weakness. Most students do not.

Those few students who acknowledge a weakness and actively address it by submitting a graded paper or writing sample are greatly admired by college admission representatives.

In many cases, these students are the ones who get into their top-choice colleges.

#38—Take Senior Standardized Tests

Why Do It
Senior year in high school marks the passing of many things that students will miss. Taking a college entrance test is probably *not* one of those things. Many students are uncomfortable with these tests. Most feel they are not an accurate reflection of their ability to do quality work in college.

Whatever your feelings about college entrance tests, most selective colleges in this country care about the results of these tests. In fact, most schools regard college entrance test scores, along with information about courses and grades, as the cornerstone on which most admission decisions are made.

With this in mind, it is time to emphasize the importance of one last set of tests. The colleges want them, you need to take them, so let's give it, pardon the pun, the old "college try."

How to Do It
A wide variety of tests will be offered during your senior year. I suggest you take the following:

- A *minimum of one SAT I*. If you are applying to colleges that do not require the SAT II, then take two SAT I exams in the fall of your senior year.
- An *SAT II if required by the colleges to which you applying*. You might have followed suggestion #14 and taken the SAT II earlier. If you did not do as well as you would have liked, consider taking the exam again, in the fall of your senior year. Speak with your college advisor and teachers to decide which SAT II you should take in the fall.
- *One last ACT test*. If you followed suggestion #24, you took your first ACT in your junior year. Now is the time to complete the testing cycle by taking your last ACT.

What You'll Get Out of It
By mid-December of your senior year, you should have taken, depending on your course load:

- two PSAT tests
- three to four SAT I tests
- one to two SAT II tests
- two ACT tests

As long as most selective colleges view these tests as an important part of the admission process, I will continue to counsel students to take them. Generally speaking, the more times you take them, the higher your scores. The higher your scores, the stronger your application. Without question, for most students, high test scores play an important role in getting into the college of their choice.

#39—Choose Carefully When Asking for Recommendations

Why Do It

Recommendations have a way of bringing an application to life. A recommendation alone probably won't get you into college. However, a recommendation could keep you from gaining admission.

Therefore, it is important to choose carefully when selecting the people who will write to the colleges on your behalf. Their words, phrases, and tone will be examined for what they say and don't say about you.

How to Do It

Here are some of the things you can do to ensure the best possible recommendations:

- Request a recommendation from someone who knows you well and has seen you perform at your best.
- Read the recommendation form carefully. It may limit the author of your recommendation letter to a teacher you studied with during the past year or to one who taught you in a major subject (English, math, science, language, etc.).
- Meet privately with the person or people you have selected and discuss your college plans. Explain how you came to select a particular school, and tell your recommender whether you have visited the campus or interviewed with an admission officer.
- Present your recommender with several items:

     your resume
     your transcript
     a stamped and addressed envelope to mail the letter directly
        to the college

- Give your recommenders enough time. Two to four weeks should do it. You may want to check back with that person as any deadline draws near.
- Always sign the "Waiver of Right to Review" line on the recommendation. By doing so, you are saying that you trust the views of the author and you have no interest in reviewing the document. If you do not sign the waiver, you run the risk that the colleges may choose to ignore everything stated in the recommendation.

- Avoid "famous person letters." Unless the famous person knows both you *and* the college, these letters are unlikely to have a positive impact on your application.

Many colleges allow you to submit recommendations from peers, parents, coaches, employers, church or community service leaders, and alumni. Try to choose people who:

- know you well
- can write honestly about you, emphasizing the positive but not ignoring your weaknesses
- can enliven the recommendations with examples and anecdotes

What You'll Get Out of It

Recommendations can be an important part of your application. If you carefully select the authors of these letters, you will have other voices representing you to these colleges, each one speaking about the many different qualities you can bring to the campus.

#40—Submit Excellent Applications

Why Do It
Your application is often the first chance an admission officer gets to "meet" you. Whether that first meeting takes place in person, on paper, or on disk, it's important that you make a good impression right from the start.

How to Do It
Here are 12 steps you can take to make your application stand out from the crowd.

---

12 Steps to Creating an Outstanding Application

1. *Read the application first.* Before starting to complete it, read the entire application thoroughly. You may think that all applications are alike (like the Common Application), but each has its own twists. By reading the application, you may come up with an idea about which of your many strengths you want to emphasize.

2. *Do it yourself.* It is perfectly natural to want others—parents, teachers, siblings, friends—to offer their perspectives on how best to complete your application. However, this is *your* application. Take total responsibility for it by drafting, writing, and mailing this document yourself.

3. *Don't lose track of time.* Note the deadlines as soon as you receive the application. It might be wise to establish a timetable for completing each application. Remember, college admission officers are likely to question your seriousness if your application is late. However, you may gain a small advantage if you submit all of your material well in advance of any deadline.

4. *Follow directions.* Directions on applications are there for a reason: to ensure that applicants are all starting on an equal footing. Always note what needs to be done, by whom, and when. You don't want your application rejected because you seem unwilling or unable to follow directions.

5. *Neatness counts.* Neatness is important at all times. When completing application questions, plan your answers carefully. Write them out on a photocopy of the application to make sure they fit in the space allowed. Don't try to scrunch your big thoughts into a small space.

---

continued

6. *Blanks are bad.* Don't leave questions blank when completing the application. Fill in all the biographical information and be sure to answer the short-answer essays (see suggestion #41).

7. *Explain your actions.* Always be complete when explaining your activities. In addition to listing the name of the organization, describe its role on campus and indicate the part you played.

8. *Support yourself.* Some colleges encourage applicants to submit material that supports or demonstrates their interest in an academic or extracurricular activity. In response, some students submit video tapes of their musical or athletic ability. Other students send art work or writing samples. Before mailing anything, call the admission office to determine the best format for your submission.

9. *One additional piece.* Many colleges give applicants the chance to supply an optional statement. After reviewing the entire application, ask yourself, "What have I not had the opportunity to tell the college about me?" You could present your thoughts on a current event or explain why this college is a good match for you.

10. *Give it a rest.* When you have completed the photocopy (never write on the original first), set it aside for a couple of days. When you pick it up again, carefully read it for errors. Ask yourself, "Am I saying what I want to say, the way I want to say it?" Share your application with trusted friends, counselors, or family members. Listen carefully to their comments and decide which changes, if any, need to be made.

11. *Copy the application.* After finalizing any changes, complete the original application. Be sure to make a photocopy of your application before you send it off.

12. Before mailing your application, check to be sure you have:
    - reviewed the application for any signatures that may be required (yours and your parents')
    - enclosed a check for the application (if required)
    - attached the proper postage for delivery

What You'll Get Out of It

Your application serves as your introduction to the college—and you want to make a good first impression. An outstanding application encourages a college to invite you into its community.

#41—Pay Attention to Short-Answer Essays

Why Do It

I have a very close friend who is a senior admission officer at one of the eight Ivy League colleges. She recently shared with me the importance placed on the responses to short-answer essays. It was her belief that the response to these questions told as much as, if not more than, the personal statement or essay. Her view was that from these responses the admission office could clearly learn which students were most serious about the college.

With this in mind, I strongly suggest you look carefully at these questions. For at least some of the most selective colleges in the country, the responses to these questions made a difference in admission for many students.

How to Do It

Here are some of the most common short-answer questions along with hints to help you frame your response to each one.

1. *"Please share with us your interest in the college."*

   Show your interest in the college through specific examples of your reasons for selecting this school. Always be positive and write as if the college were very important to you.

2. *"Please name a favorite book, movie, or author."*

   Don't try to impress the reader by writing about some esoteric book or movie that you don't really care about. Write from the heart.

3. *"Are there any special circumstances you would like to share with us?"*

   Don't make excuses. Don't create any special conditions and definitely do not make any excuses for poor performances. If there really are extenuating circumstances, however, this is a great opportunity to explain any shortcomings on your record.

4. *"Please share with us your future plans."*

   You do not have to know what you want to do with the rest of your life *before* you enroll in college. There is nothing wrong with not having selected a particular occupation or career. If you do have some ideas, don't hesitate to share them.

One final comment on this topic: Always edit your work. Your writing skills on these short-answer essays should be just as carefully reviewed as on the longer essay. Think carefully before writing and ask for comments from a parent, counselor, or teacher.

What You'll Get Out of It

Because admission officers value the written word, responses to the short-answer essays are becoming more critical to many of the most selective colleges in the country.

Answering these questions in a thoughtful, honest, and complete manner can help to strengthen your applications to your top-choice colleges.

#42—Write Strong Personal Statements/Essays

Why Do It

Whatever the application may call it (the essay, personal statement, or self-descriptive paragraph), this is the part of the application that many students fear the most. This fear is understandable when you consider that many people view writing as a chore and regard writing about themselves as a form of torture.

It's a good idea to view the essay as a chance to talk, on paper, about the subject of your choice. Unlike other parts of the application where you're given questions you *must* answer, most applications offer you a choice of essays. This should be viewed as an *opportunity* for you to select the topic that most interests you. Use your essay to tell admission professionals who you are and why you would make a very welcome addition to their college community.

How to Do It

As you write your college application essays, keep these ten guidelines in mind.

Essay Guidelines

1. *Remember, there is no right or wrong answer.* The admission committee will be assessing your writing skills, maturity, and commitment. Think about your life to date. Consider your goals, values, education, family, and future. Try to capture a sense of what's important to you, and bring that sense to the essay.

2. *Be genuine, honest, and sincere.* Select the essay option that feels right to you. If you have only one question available, it is probably very broad and will let you express yourself in a wide variety of ways.

3. *Answer the question.* Each essay question is a chance to share your views on a particular subject. Answer the question that is asked. Don't use the essay as a chance to be cute or bizarre. There is a good chance that the reader of the essay may not share your sense of taste or humor.

4. *Write naturally.* It is always a good idea to write in language that is natural for you. Simple sentences that capture your meaning are

continues

continued

very effective. Don't go running to the dictionary and thesaurus, thinking you will impress the reader with a string of big words.

5. *Give yourself plenty of time.* Organize your writing so that you can be creative, honest, and thorough, without being rushed. Don't procrastinate. In most cases, last-minute work reads as if it were thrown together quickly with little thought and little care. Give yourself time to present who you are.

6. *Use TRIS (Topic, Restriction, Illustration, Summary) whenever possible:*

   • *Topic.* State what you are going to write about. It can be as simple as restating the question.
   • *Restriction.* Essay questions often cover a great deal of ground, but you are expected to answer in only 500 words. That means you must restrict your answer to a particular part of the question.
   • *Illustration.* Simply put, you state what you have to say about the restricted topic, and then illustrate your point with an example or a fact.
   • *Summary.* After you make your point, summarize it by relating it to the point of your essay.

7. *Edit, edit, edit.* Take out extraneous words or incoherent thoughts. Don't ramble and don't repeat yourself. Write a draft and then rewrite, rewrite, rewrite.

8. *Read it aloud.* Always take the time to read your essay slowly and out loud to yourself. By doing so, you'll spot subtle mistakes (like sloppy grammar, disjointed sentences, etc.). You will also note the flow from idea to idea, and you can check to see if your personality comes through.

9. *Check for neatness, grammar, and punctuation.* Remember, your application represents you. Sloppiness and grammar/punctuation errors detract from even the best thought-out essays.

10. *Show your work to others.* When you're fairly satisfied with your essay, share it with those who will give you honest feedback. Listen carefully to their views; then decide what changes (if any) you want to make. After all, who knows you better than you?

What You'll Get Out of It

Simply put, the essay is your voice. Why would you want to show admission officers anything other than the real you?

The rest of your application represents you in a statistical way (grades, scores, and listings of activities). The essay in your own voice helps to bring all the dry statistical information to life.

#43—Consider a Cover Letter

Why Do It
In reviewing your completed application, you might want to consider the idea of drawing particular attention to certain parts that either exhibit strength or need further explanation. Let's face it: No one is perfect. Things happen that need explanation. If the application does not offer you the opportunity to explain your situation, you need to find another way to communicate these issues to the admission office.

If you feel the need to explain (not excuse, but explain) something about your academic record, extracurricular activities, or family circumstances, consider doing so in a letter to be attached to the front of your application.

How to Do It
Remember to make the letter specific to your particular situation. A sample letter might look something like this:

Your name
Your street address
Your town, state, ZIP code
Your telephone number

Date

Dear Admission Committee:

I am writing you today to share some aspects of myself that I feel you and others at the college might find helpful when evaluating my application to _____ University.

As you can clearly see from my academic record, I got off to a difficult start in high school. At the time I entered high school, I was simply not motivated to work hard and earn good grades. I do not share this with you as an excuse, but rather as an explanation for my poor grades.

In my sophomore year, I decided to focus my attention on my grades. By the end of my junior year, I was named a member of the National Honor Society. My standardized test scores of 1200 on the SAT and 28 on the ACT also reflect my academic ability.

The extracurricular activities I have listed on my application are many and varied. I am especially proud of my community service efforts and holding down a 20-hour-per-week job. Both of these interests indicate that I am comfortable in making a contribution beyond my school.

I would also like to share my serious interest in _____ University. I met (name of person here), your admission representative, during my wonderful visit

continues

---

continued

to campus last fall. Since that time, we have spoken on the telephone in an effort to update each other. She has been a major reason why I am so excited about your institution.

As I said at the outset of this letter, I simply wanted to share with you some aspects of myself. I hope you give me the chance to join your community next fall.

Sincerely,

Your name

What You'll Get Out of It

Despite what you may hear and fear, admission officers are human. At many selective colleges, they have a truly difficult job deciding which students to admit from so many outstanding applicants.

If there is something less than outstanding about your application, these officers will find it. So why not beat the admission officer to the punch with an honest explanation of any weakness in your record? If you are sincere about the circumstances, it can only help your case.

#44—Share Another Side of Yourself

Why Do It

In recent years, some students have supplemented their applications with items to catch the attention of the admission office. Many such items support the application by reflecting abilities that have been developed over many years. These are positive additions to the application and should have a positive impact on the decision.

Other students have taken this concept too far, attempting to use "gimmicks" to gain admission. This approach rarely works. In fact, it often "cheapens" a solid applicant's application.

Some students may have difficulty differentiating between positive and negative supplements. A good rule of thumb is to ask yourself this question: Is what I am sharing something that reflects my interests, talents, and hard work? If the answer is yes, then share it. If not, save it for a rainy day—after you are admitted.

How to Do It

Here are examples of potentially positive and negative items to share in the admission process:

Potentially Positive Items

- Anything that illustrates a long-term hobby or avocation
- Audio- or videotapes of original music
- Audio- or videotapes of a music performance
- Videotapes of an extensive collection
- Anything that is truly significant to you and is a clear reflection of you

Potentially Negative Items

- Videotaped love letters to the college
- A shoe with a note, "Now that I have one foot in the door . . ."
- A medicine bottle with a prescription that reads, "Applicant needs four years at (whatever college)"
- A photograph of the applicant painting his/her room (whatever college) colors
- The school seal made of chocolate
- A life raft with a note that says, "Save me by admitting me to (whatever college)"
- The entire application written backward

What You'll Get Out of It

There is a difference between sharing something that is representative of a talent, interest, or ability, and trying to be cute. Cute rarely works. Share something that reflects you and what you care about, and admission officers are much more likely to appreciate your efforts by finding a spot for you in the freshman class.

#45—Follow Up on Your Applications

Why Do It

I'll tell you a secret. One of my worst nightmares recurs every year at admission time. I dream that the wonderful applications sent by my students never arrive at the colleges. Rather, they are lost forever on some boat, plane, or truck.

The most frightening thing about this situation is that you never learn about it until it's too late. The freshman class is selected, and my student sits waiting for an answer that will never come because the application never arrived.

When it comes to college applications arriving safely at their destination, never assume anything. Many colleges receive over 100,000 parts of applications. To assume that all of those pieces arrive safe and sound is a pretty big leap of faith.

Instead of assuming anything, I strongly suggest that you follow up on each application to make sure all of your material arrives in a timely manner. Wouldn't it be a shame to submit a great application and not gain admission simply because you failed to follow through and determine whether your application had arrived?

How to Do It

There are six important things you should do immediately before and within 2–3 weeks after applying to college.

Application Follow-Up

1. Always photocopy your part of the applications before mailing. It's a good idea to ask those writing recommendations to do the same.
2. Complete any return postcards and mail with your application. Colleges will return these cards after processing your application.
3. Within 2–3 weeks after submitting your applications, telephone each college and ask whether your application and *all* supporting materials have been received.
4. Make a note of the date, time, and person you spoke with regarding your application.

continues

continued

5. If material is missing, start to gather copies from your files and teachers.
6. After another week, reconnect with the person you spoke with before to determine if the material was found. In many cases, it simply wasn't processed yet.

What You'll Get Out of It

The habit of following up on a job is often the difference between a job done and a job well done. All the time, energy, and effort you put in on your application are certainly worth a phone call to make sure it arrives at its destination.

Students who follow up on their applications are more likely to find themselves members of the freshmen class at the college of their choice.

#46—Send Copies of Your Application to a Few Special People

Why Do It

Once you have completed your application, you might consider sending a copy to certain select individuals who are "well connected" with either you or the institutions to which you are applying.

Their influence may not get you admitted, but it is not likely to have a negative impact on your application.

How to Do It

Here's what you'll have to do to identify and enlist the help of these "special" people who might assist you in the final stages of the admission process:

1. Identify those who could assist you. Think about the many people you have come in fairly close contact with throughout the application process. These people might include:

    *   the admission office interviewer
    *   the admission officer who conducted the group session
    *   the admission representative who visited your high school
    *   the admission officer you met at a college fair
    *   the admission officer you met at the campus open house
    *   the faculty member you spoke with at length when visiting the campus
    *   the graduate who encouraged you to explore the particular college
    *   the coach you spoke with or wrote to on several occasions
    *   a friend who graduated from a college to which you are applying

2. Request their assistance by letter. You might want to say something like this:

    Because you are in the unique position of knowing both the college and me, I want to ask if you would consider supporting my candidacy at (name of college)? To that end, I would like to request your assistance in gaining admission.

    I would be most appreciative if you would allow me to forward a copy of my application to you. Anything your could or would do to support my candidacy at (name of college) would be most welcome.

3. Make copies of your application (including the essays) and your transcript (all courses, grades, and scores).

4. Send these copies of your application to those who respond to your request for help. Be sure to include a note specifying the due date for your recommendations.

What You'll Get Out of It

When I was representing a particular college, I cannot tell you how many times I wondered about the admission results of a particular student. Because I interviewed the student, some might assume that I would also naturally review and evaluate the application for admission. In many cases, that was not the case.

On those occasions when I was contacted by a student I had interviewed, I quickly made sure the file was routed by me so that I could express my opinions. More often than not, by receiving "additional" attention, those students gained admission.

#47—Update Your File

Why Do It

It is incorrect to assume that your responsibilities are over when you mail the application. Although only a very few students actually send an "update" to their colleges after applying, those few students who do, give two very distinct impressions:

1. They continue to be active in high school. Typically, colleges like active students.
2. They truly care about the college. Students who care are more likely to attend the college if offered the chance to do so.

How to Do It

The steps are quite simple but very important:

1. If a college submits a follow-up form, complete it and send it by the date listed.
2. If no form is included, send a letter to the college in a timely manner. Remember, you don't want to wait until the admission decision has been made. In fact, because timing is important, you might want to contact the colleges and ask by what date they need an update.
3. Include these items in your update:
   - most recent grade reports
   - most recent standardized score reports
   - additional academic honors from your high school
   - additional extracurricular activity honors at school
   - a promotion at work
4. If you have narrowed your "top choice" college(s) to one or two (and this college is one of them), you would want to include that information.

What You'll Get Out of It

Knowing that admission officers generally subscribe to the theory that "information is powerful," the student who provides the most comprehensive picture of himself or herself is the person most admission officers want as a member of their community.

#48—Contact Friends Attending Your Favorite Colleges

Why Do It
Students currently attending a particular college are likely to be listened to by their admission offices. While a student's recommendation might not carry the same weight as that of a billionaire benefactor, students' perspectives on possible future members of their college community are rarely ignored.

You may want to consider contacting any friends currently attending colleges to which you are applying. The better these friends know you, the more they can help your cause.

How to Do It
Here's what you can do:

1. Ask yourself, "How well do I know this person?" If the answer is fairly well, then proceed. If not, drop the idea.
2. Ask the friend if he or she would consider writing a letter to the college on your behalf. If the answer is positive, proceed quickly.
3. Provide the friend with a copy of your resume, your application and essays, and your transcript.
4. Meet with the friend and share:
   - why you want to attend the college (be fairly specific)
   - your involvement to date with the college (interviews and tours)
   - your intended major and extracurricular interests
   - your future goals and plans
5. Ask your friend to write a letter supporting your candidacy.
6. Once you have submitted the letter, send a thank-you note, small gift, etc., to your friend.

What You'll Get Out of It
Colleges are communities with a common bond—the desire to grow and thrive. One good way to keep a community moving forward is to encourage members of the community to feel that they can have input into the composition of the future community. While there are no guarantees that a student recommendation will get you in, you certainly can't hurt your chances by having a strong supporter in your corner.

#49—Interview with a Local Graduate

Why Do It

One last voice that might help to get your message across to the admission office is that of a local graduate who volunteers a few hours each year to interview prospective candidates for admission. If you are unable or can't afford to visit the college, these alumni interviewers may be the only representatives you will meet. The opinions of these volunteers tend to be listened to very closely by the admission office.

Frankly, you can't know how any local graduate interviewer is viewed by the college admission office, so the best advice is to treat any interview seriously and prepare accordingly.

How to Do It

As with the interview on campus, there are certain things you can do to make your interview a very positive experience.

Make the Most of Your Interview

1. *Do your homework.* Thoroughly research the college before arrival.
2. *Arrive early.* If you have five minutes to spare before the scheduled interview, you'll feel less rushed and more comfortable when the interview starts.
3. *Greet the interviewer with a firm handshake.* It expresses confidence.
4. *Bring materials with you.* Come prepared with questions, a resume, and your latest transcript.
5. *Get comfortable.* Relax and be prepared to listen and share.
6. *Enjoy yourself.* You are the center of attention, so enjoy it.
7. *Speak directly to the interviewer.* Remember that making eye contact is important.
8. *Open your mouth and talk.* Now is the time to share.
9. *Be yourself.* The interviewer is not looking for anyone other than you.
10. *Know the three most common interview questions and be prepared to answer them.* See suggestion #26.

What You'll Get Out of It

Unlike the campus interview, where you are fairly sure to speak with a member of the decision-making team, the interview with a local graduate may or may not have an impact on your application for admission.

My experience tells me that it is always best to conclude that every contact in the admission process is important and may play an important part in the decision on your file. If the volunteer interviewer writes a glowing report, the admission officers may feel they simply must have you as a member of their community.

#50—Explore Other Options

Why Do It

The premise of this book is that there are "Things" you can do to get into the college of your choice. Let's suppose they didn't work for you because of one of these reasons:

- You started using these ideas too late in your senior year for them to help.
- You bought the book but didn't use any of these suggestions.
- You used a few, but not very seriously.

As a result, you didn't gain admission to institutions that really excite you. You're not pleased and don't know where to turn.

Relax for a moment. You do have options. There are still things you can do over the next few months to gain admission to the college of your choice.

How to Do It

There are five options available for you to try to reach your objective:

1. *Attend another college.* If you were not admitted to any of the colleges you would most like to attend, but you did gain admission to a college or two, you might want to consider selecting one of those colleges and attending. You might be quite surprised and enjoy it.

2. *Apply as a transfer student.* If, after attending one complete semester or more at college, you still think you would be happier at a different school, consider applying as a transfer student. To gain admission as a transfer student, you need to earn good grades, and you'll have to start the entire admission process again.

3. *Attend a two-year college.* These colleges are specifically designed to assist students who want to transfer to a four-year college. They are good options for many students in that:

   - they are usually much less expensive than four-year colleges
   - you can explore a variety of academic options
   - the academic credits you earn can transfer to four-year colleges
   - classes are held both day and night so you can hold down a job

4. *Take the year off.* After exploring your options, you may decide to take a year off because you want to:
   - make money through employment
   - explore different careers
   - help others through community service
   - gain some perspective or maturity through any of the above

5. *Explore a postgraduate year.* Many private high schools offer students the option of taking an additional year of high school in order to:
   - improve their grades
   - increase their credit hours
   - enhance their standardized test scores
   - gain some maturity

After exploring any one of these five options, you may then find yourself better prepared to apply and gain admission to the college of your choice.

What You'll Get Out of It

There is no rule stating that you have to go from high school straight to college. Some students need more time. My suggestion is to take the time if you need it; and if college remains your goal, perhaps with added maturity you will find what you are looking for. If this book has helped you in your journey, then I am honored to have played a small role.

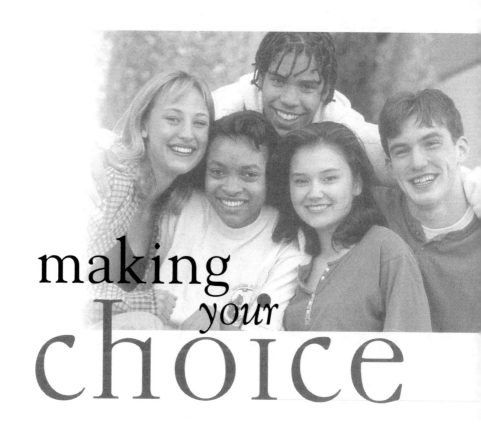

making *your* choice

selecting the "best" college option

The college responses have arrived. You have sorted through the admission offers and narrowed the choices to a few colleges. This is the big decision. Which college should you select? Rather than base your choice on stale information from months gone by, you should consider visiting each campus one last time in order to reach a decision based on your present view of these college options.

When you first started your journal, you were just beginning the application process. Back then, you were probably more interested in leaving a good impression than in getting a clear picture of the college. Now the roles are reversed. The college needs to make a positive impression on you.

Some counselors don't recommend that parents accompany students on these return trips. But, as long as the student realizes that the decision is his or hers to make and the parents are willing to support that decision, the trip can be an opportunity for the parents to offer their views, the student to exercise decision-making skills, and the family to enjoy one last official college road trip together.

Before you set out on this trip, review your journal entries from your prior college visits. This is the time to ask yourself particular questions about your previous visits:

- What were the features about each of the colleges that meant the most to you?
- What were your positive feelings about the college?
- What features impressed you the least?
- What words did you use to describe the college?

When you review these questions, a picture emerges about the college. Is this picture an accurate one? How does this picture compare with the pictures of other college options? Do you notice a change from the way you viewed certain colleges then, to the way you view them now?

Revisiting the Colleges

Contact the admission offices and arrange for some or all of the meetings described in the following list. Regardless of what you did or did not do on your preceding visit, this visit should include explorations of all of the following:

- **Financial Aid Office**
  Make an appointment before you visit. This meeting should include a detailed discussion of your financial aid offer, payment dates and options, loan terms, college work-study options, and any additional questions you or your parents might have. It is important to leave the office knowing what is due, when it is due, and whom to speak with if questions arise.

- **Academic Program**
  Work with the admission office to schedule an appointment with a faculty member in the department of your major. Ask the professor about:

      student/faculty advising efforts
      class selection and scheduling
      your particular major
      research projects with professors

  In general, try to determine whether this is a program where you will be challenged and your interest maintained.

- **Housing Office**
  Ask about the different housing options, costs, locations, roommate selection procedure, etc. If you can choose your housing, ask whether you can tour the facilities before you make your selection. If possible, try to spend the evening in a residence hall.

- **Your Particular Interests**
  This includes meeting with coaches, theater/music/dance faculty, and club and organization sponsors. If you have a favorite high school activity that you might want to continue in college, now is the time to check out facilities and opportunities.
- **Eating Options**
  By all means, eat your meals on campus. Make sure that you are familiar with the different meal plans, costs, variety, and locations of the food services on campus.
- **Campus Environment**
  Try to get a sense of the campus both during the day and at night. Is the campus located in a safe and secure environment? What is the relationship with the "townies"?
- **Off-Campus Stuff**
  What social and extracurricular options are available in the area surrounding the campus? Do students take advantage of these opportunities?

While you may have explored some of these issues during your initial visit, you are now seeing them through the eyes of a new member of the community. Things *will* look different with your new "I'll be here for four more years" perspective.

Once you have revisited the colleges that interest you most, you'll have to make the final decision on which one you will attend. Before reaching any final conclusion, you might want to focus on these six final points:

1. **Don't rush—but know your real deadline.**
   Some colleges may try to push you into making a decision before the Candidate's Reply Date of May 1. Unless you chose an "Early" application program that committed you to attending if admitted, you are by no means required to decide until May 1.

2. **Talk to others—but listen to yourself.**
   It's a good idea to get the perspective of others you trust before you make a final decision. Talk to:

   > parents and other family members
   > graduates
   > current college students
   > classmates
   > high school teachers
   > guidance counselor

Get as many opinions as you can, but remember: *You are the one going to college—and in the end, you are the one who must make the decision for yourself.*

3. **Read and reread everything you can find about the colleges.**
   Review both objective and subjective material about your final choices. Examine viewbooks and catalogs, and reread the journal you kept during college visits.

4. **Review your college-selection criteria.**
   The criteria you selected several months ago may well have changed as you accumulated more college information and made more college visits. Think carefully about these changes. What caused the change? Sometimes certain college features become much less important to you once you put them in perspective. Now is the time for deep thought and reflection.

5. **Examine your reasons for reaching your decision.**
   Here are some things that could affect your college choice:

   > cost, affordability, and financial aid
   > accessiblity of faculty
   > outstanding academic programs in your major area
   > great social life on campus
   > great social life off campus
   > small classes with lots of individual attention
   > extensive winter break (starts before Thanksgiving)
   > beautiful campus
   > peaceful (or exciting) surrounding area
   > nearness to family/friends/someone special
   > distance from family/friends/someone special

6. **Trust your heart.**
   After you've talked with those you trust, read viewbooks and catalogs until your eyes ache, and thought over and over about what you want and need from a college, ask yourself a few final questions:

   - How do you truly feel about each college?
   - Where do you see yourself being happiest?
   - Where do you see yourself being most challenged?
   - Where will you feel most at home?

When you take all of these points into account, one school will emerge as the best choice for you. GO FOR IT!

author's
choice

In the pages that follow, I share the results of extensive reading and literally thousands of conversations with college representatives that have taken place over the last 17 years. The topics covered range from the strongest academic programs, the best college towns, the "hottest" and "safest" colleges, and the friendliest students to the most diverse student bodies, the most extensive fraternity and sorority programs, and a listing of my favorite colleges.

The ratings that follow are based on these conversations and *my* personal opinions. The institutions named are in alphabetical order. I hope you find these lists a useful starting point for further research on your part.

COLLEGES WITH PARTICULARLY STRONG ACADEMIC PROGRAMS IN...

Accounting
Bentley College (MA)
College of William and Mary (VA)
Duquesne University (PA)
Fordham University (NY)
Hofstra University (NY)
John Carroll University (OH)
Santa Clara University (CA)
Transylvania University (KY)
University of Denver (CO)
University of Illinois (IL)
University of Notre Dame (IN)
University of Richmond (VA)
University of San Diego (CA)
Wake Forest University (NC)

Agriculture
Auburn University (AL)
Colorado State University (CO)
Cornell University (NY)
Iowa State University (IA)
Ohio State University (OH)
Pennsylvania State University (PA)
Purdue University (IN)
Texas A&M University (TX)
University of California at Davis (CA)
University of Kentucky (KY)
University of Maine (ME)
University of Missouri (MO)

Anthropology
Beloit College (WI)
Grinnell College (IA)
Macalester College (MN)
Pitzer College (CA)

University of Chicago (IL)
University of Florida (FL)
University of Washington (WA)

Architecture
Arizona State University (AZ)
Auburn University (AL)
Ball State University (IN)
Carnegie Mellon University (PA)
Catholic University (DC)
Clemson University (SC)
The Cooper Union for the Advancement
   of Science and Art (NY)
Georgia Institute of Technology (GA)
Princeton University (NJ)
Rice University (TX)
Tulane University (LA)
University of Kansas (KS)
University of Notre Dame (IN)
University of Oregon (OR)
University of Southern California
   (CA)

Art History
Bryn Mawr College (PA)
Case Western Reserve University (OH)
Columbia University (NY)
Hollins College (VA)
New York University (NY)
Smith College (MA)
Sweet Briar College (VA)
University of Rochester (NY)
Washington University (MO)
Wellesley College (MA)
Williams College (MA)

Biology

Agnes Scott College (GA)
Albion College (MI)
Alma College (MI)
Bates College (ME)
Bowdoin College (ME)
Colby College (ME)
College of Charleston (SC)
College of William and Mary (VA)
Drake University (IA)
Earlham College (IN)
Franklin and Marshall College (PA)
Furman University (SC)
Grinnell College (IA)
Gustavus Adolphus College (MN)
Harvard University (MA)
Hendrix College (AR)
Hiram College (OH)
Hope College (MI)
Indiana University (IN)
Johns Hopkins University (MD)
Juniata College (PA)
Kalamazoo College (MI)
Knox College (IL)
Macalester College (MN)
Marquette University (WI)
Ripon College (WI)
Swarthmore College (PA)
Texas Christian University (TX)
Trinity University (TX)
Tufts University (MA)
University of California at Davis (CA)
University of California at Irvine (CA)
University of Chicago (IL)
University of Georgia (GA)
University of North Carolina at Chapel
  Hill (NC)
University of Richmond (VA)
University of Rochester (NY)
University of Texas (TX)
University of the South (TN)

Ursinus College (PA)
Washington and Jefferson College (PA)

Business Administration

American University (DC)
Auburn University (AL)
Babson College (MA)
Bentley College (MA)
Bucknell University (PA)
Butler University (IN)
Case Western Reserve University (OH)
College of William and Mary (VA)
DePaul University (IL)
Drake University (IA)
Georgetown University (DC)
Howard University (DC)
Indiana University (IN)
James Madison University (VA)
Lehigh University (PA)
Loyola Marymount University (CA)
Miami University (OH)
Michigan State University (MI)
Morehouse College (GA)
New York University (NY)
Northeastern University (MA)
Ohio State University (OH)
Ohio Weselyan University (OH)
Pennsylvania State University (PA)
Pepperdine University (CA)
Providence College (RI)
Saint Joseph's College (IN)
Saint Mary's College (IN)
Texas Christian University (TX)
Transylvania University (KY)
Trinity University (TX)
University of California at Berkeley (CA)
University of Colorado (CO)
University of Connecticut (CT)
University of Dayton (OH)
University of Delaware (DE)

University of Denver (CO)
University of Georgia (GA)
University of Hartford (CT)
University of Michigan (MI)
University of Notre Dame (IN)
University of Oregon (OR)
University of Pennsylvania (PA)
University of South Carolina (SC)
University of Vermont (VT)
University of Virginia (VA)
University of Wisconsin (WI)
Ursinus College (PA)
Villanova University (PA)
Wagner College (NY)
Wake Forest University (NC)

Chemistry

Albion College (MI)
Brandeis University (MA)
Brown University (RI)
Carleton College (MN)
Case Western Reserve University (OH)
College of Charleston (SC)
College of Wooster (OH)
Cornell College (IA)
Dartmouth College (NH)
Furman University (SC)
Grinnell College (IA)
Gustavus Adolphus College (MN)
Harvey Mudd College (CA)
Hendrix College (AR)
Hope College (MI)
Indiana University (IN)
Johns Hopkins University (MD)
Juniata College (PA)
Kalamazoo College (MI)
Knox College (IL)
Lawrence University (WI)
Macalester College (MN)
Occidental College (CA)
Ohio Northern University (OH)

Reed College (OR)
Saint Olaf College (MN)
Spelman College (GA)
Stanford University (CA)
Trinity University (TX)
Union College (NY)
University of California at Berkeley (CA)
University of Delaware (DE)
University of Illinois (IL)
University of North Carolina at Chapel
    Hill (NC)
University of Notre Dame (IN)
University of Richmond (VA)
University of Rochester (NY)
Ursinus College (PA)
Washington and Jefferson College (PA)
Washington University (MO)
Williams College (MA)

Classics

Bryn Mawr College (PA)
Catholic University (DC)
Centre College (KY)
College of Holy Cross (MA)
Columbia University (NY)
Fordham University (NY)
Gustavus Adolphus College (MN)
Middlebury College (VT)
Ripon College (WI)
University of Chicago (IL)
University of Michigan (MI)
University of North Carolina at Chapel
    Hill (NC)
Wabash College (IN)

Computer Science

Arizona State University (AZ)
Brown University (RI)
Carnegie Mellon University (PA)
Cornell University (NY)

Dartmouth College (NH)
DePaul University (IL)
Drexel University (PA)
Georgia Institute of Technology (GA)
Massachusetts Institute of Technology (MA)
Pennsylvania State University (PA)
Rensselaer Polytechnic Institute (NY)
Rochester Institute of Technology (NY)
Stanford University (CA)
University of Illinois (IL)
University of Texas (TX)
Worcester Institute of Technology (MA)

Economics

Albion College (MI)
Brandeis University (MA)
Bucknell University (PA)
Claremont McKenna College (CA)
Colby College (ME)
Denison University (OH)
DePauw University (IN)
Duke University (NC)
Guilford College (NC)
Hamilton College (NY)
Hampden-Sydney College (VA)
Harvard University (MA)
Hendrix College (AR)
Lafayette College (PA)
Macalester College (MN)
Rhodes College (TN)
Smith College (MA)
St. Lawrence University (NY)
Trinity University (TX)
United States Military Academy at West Point (NY)
University of Chicago (IL)
University of Michigan (MI)
University of Oregon (OR)
University of Virginia (VA)
Wabash College (IN)

Washington and Lee University (VA)
Wesleyan University (CT)
Wheaton College (MA)

Education

Adrian College (MI)
Ball State University (IN)
Boston University (MA)
Indiana University (IN)
James Madison University (VA)
Ohio State University (OH)
Pennsylvania State University (PA)
Saint Joseph's College (IN)
Saint Mary's College (IN)
Seton Hall University (NJ)
University of Kentucky (KY)
University of Northern Colorado (CO)
Vanderbilt University (TN)

Engineering

Bucknell University (PA)
California Institute of Technology (CA)
Carnegie Mellon University (PA)
Clarkson University (NY)
Clemson University (SC)
Colorado School of Mines (CO)
The Cooper Union for the Advancement of Science and Art (NY)
Cornell University (NY)
Drexel University (PA)
Georgia Institute of Technology (GA)
GMI Engineering Institute (MI)
Grove City College (PA)
Iowa State University (IA)
Johns Hopkins University (MD)
Lehigh University (PA)
Massachusetts Institute of Technology (MA)
Ohio State University (OH)
Pennsylvania State University (PA)

Purdue University (IN)

Rensselaer Polytechnic Institute (NY)

Rice University (TX)

Rochester Institute of Technology (NY)

Rose-Hulman Institute of Technology (IN)

Santa Clara University (CA)

Texas A&M University (TX)

United States Air Force Academy at Colorado Springs (CO)

United States Coast Guard Academy at New London (CT)

United States Military Academy at West Point (NY)

United States Naval Academy at Annapolis (MD)

University of California at Berkeley (CA)

University of California at Los Angeles (CA)

University of Colorado (CO)

University of Connecticut (CT)

University of Dayton (OH)

University of Delaware (DE)

University of Illinois (IL)

University of Kansas (KS)

University of Michigan (MI)

University of Texas (TX)

University of Washington (WA)

Virginia Military Institute (VA)

Virginia Polytechnic Institute and State University (VA)

Worcester Polytechnic Institute (MA)

English

Allegheny College (PA)

Barnard College (NY)

Centre College (KY)

Chatham College (PA)

Colorado College (CO)

Cornell College (IA)

Dartmouth College (NH)

Dickinson College (PA)

Earlham College (IN)

Goucher College (MD)

Guilford College (NC)

Hanover College (IN)

Haverford College (PA)

Hendrix College (AR)

Hollins College (VA)

Kalamazoo College (MI)

Kenyon College (OH)

Knox College (IL)

Middlebury College (VT)

Millsaps College (MS)

Oglethorpe University (GA)

Reed College (OR)

Rice University (TX)

Smith College (MA)

Spelman College (GA)

State University of New York at Binghamton (NY)

Sweet Briar College (VA)

Trinity College (CT)

Trinity University (TX)

University of California at Berkeley (CA)

University of Chicago (IL)

University of Iowa (IA)

University of Michigan (MI)

University of New Hampshire (NH)

University of North Carolina at Chapel Hill (NC)

University of Oregon (OR)

University of the South (TN)

University of Virginia (VA)

Wabash College (IN)

Washington and Lee University (VA)

Whitman College (WA)

Yale University (CT)

Environmental Science/Studies

Bowdoin College (ME)
Cornell University (NY)
Middlebury College (VT)
Oregon State University (OR)
Pennsylvania State University (PA)
St. Lawrence University (NY)
University of California at Santa
    Barbara (CA)
University of California at Santa Cruz
    (CA)
University of Colorado (CO)
University of Florida (FL)
University of Vermont (VT)
University of Washington (WA)

Film Studies

Columbia University (NY)
Ithaca College (NY)
New York University (NY)
Northwestern University (IL)
Syracuse University (NY)
Temple University (PA)
University of California at Los Angeles
    (CA)
University of Michigan (MI)
University of Southern California (CA)

Geology

Beloit University (WI)
Colorado College (CO)
Trinity Univeristy (TX)

Government/Political Science

American University (DC)
Bowdoin College (ME)
Claremont McKenna College (CA)

Colby College (ME)
College of William and Mary (VA)
Colorado College (CO)
Dartmouth College (NH)
DePauw University (IN)
Emory College (GA)
George Washington University (DC)
Georgetown University (DC)
Hampden-Sydney College (VA)
Harvard University (MA)
Marquette University (WI)
Rutgers University (NJ)
Smith College (MA)
State University of New York at
    Albany (NY)
Sweet Briar College (VA)
United States Military Academy at
    West Point (NY)
University of Michigan (MI)
University of Notre Dame (IN)
University of the South (TN)
University of Virginia (VA)
University of Wisconsin (WI)
Wabash College (IN)
Washington and Jefferson College (PA)
Whitman College (WA)
Willamette University (OR)

History

College of Charleston (SC)
College of William and Mary (VA)
College of Wooster (OH)
Colorado College (CO)
Davidson College (NC)
Duke University (NC)
Guilford College (NC)
Hampden-Sydney College (VA)
Hanover College (IN)
Hollins College (VA)
Lawrence University (WI)
Macalester College (MN)

Marquette University (WI)
Ohio University (OH)
Princeton University (NJ)
Reed College (OR)
Rice University (TX)
Ripon College (WI)
Trinity College (CT)
Trinity University (TX)
Union College (NY)
University of Michigan (MI)
University of North Carolina at Chapel Hill (NC)
University of the South (TN)
University of Virginia (VA)
Wabash College (IN)
Wake Forest University (NC)
Washington and Jefferson College (PA)
Washington and Lee University (VA)
Whitman College (WA)
Yale University (CT)

Hospitality/Hotel Management

Berea College (KY)
Cornell University (NY)
Transylvania University (KY)
University of Denver (CO)
University of Nevada at Las Vegas (NV)
University of New Hampshire (NH)

International Relations

Alma College (MI)
Claremont McKenna College (CA)
Eckerd College (FL)
George Washington University (DC)
Georgetown University (DC)
Johns Hopkins University (MD)
Kalamazoo College (MI)
Lehigh University (PA)
Lewis and Clark College (OR)

Middlebury College (VT)
Princeton University (NJ)
Rhodes College (TN)
Tufts University (MA)
Tulane University (LA)
University of South Carolina (SC)
University of Washington (WA)

Journalism/ Communications

Butler University (IN)
DePauw University (IN)
Drake University (IA)
Hofstra University (NY)
Indiana University (IN)
Ithaca College (NY)
James Madison University (VA)
Miami University (OH)
Northwestern University (IL)
Ohio University (OH)
Syracuse University (NY)
Temple University (PA)
Trinity University (TX)
University of California at Los Angeles (CA)
University of Georgia (GA)
University of Iowa (IA)
University of Kansas (KS)
University of Michigan (MI)
University of Missouri (MO)
University of North Carolina at Chapel Hill (NC)
University of Oregon (OR)
University of Southern California (CA)
University of Wisconsin (WI)

Languages

Barnard College (NY)
Dartmouth College (NH)
Dickinson College (PA)

Earlham College (IN)

Emory University (GA)

Georgetown University (DC)

Indiana University (IN)

Middlebury College (VT)

Mills College (CA)

Mount Holyoke University (MA)

United States Military Academy at West Point (NY)

University of California at Berkeley (CA)

University of Chicago (IL)

University of Texas (TX)

Washington University (MO)

Marine Biology

Eckerd College (FL)

Florida Institute of Technology (FL)

University of California at Santa Cruz (CA)

University Of Miami (FL)

Mathematics

Albion College (MI)

California Institute of Technology (CA)

Case Western Reserve University (OH)

Centre College (KY)

Dartmouth College (NH)

Fisk University (TN)

Harvey Mudd College (CA)

Massachusetts Institute of Technology (MA)

New York University (NY)

Rochester Institute of Technology (NY)

St. Olaf College (MN)

Trinity University (TX)

Union College (NY)

University of Chicago (IL)

University of Colorado (CO)

University of Michigan (MI)

University of Rochester (NY)

University of the South (TN)

Washington University (MO)

Music

Butler University (IN)

Carnegie Mellon University (PA)

Catholic University (DC)

Connecticut College (CT)

DePauw University (IN)

Eastman School of Music (NY)

Florida State University (FL)

Harvard University (MA)

Indiana University (IN)

Ithaca College (NY)

Juilliard School (NY)

Lawrence University (WI)

Millikin University (IL)

Mills College (CA)

Northwestern University (IL)

Oberlin College (OH)

Skidmore College (NY)

St. Olaf University (MN)

University of California at Los Angeles (CA)

University of Colorado (CO)

University of Denver (CO)

University of Iowa (IA)

University of Kansas (KS)

University of Miami (FL)

University of Michigan (MI)

University of Northern Colorado (CO)

University of Oregon (OR)

Willamette University (OR)

Yale University (CT)

Nursing

Boston College (MA)

Case Western University (OH)

Duquesne University (PA)

Georgetown University (DC)
Mount St. Mary's College (CA)
Northeastern University (MA)
Ohio State University (OH)
Purdue University (IN)
Saint Anselm College (NH)
Saint Mary's College (IN)
Simmons College (MA)
University of Evansville (IN)
University of Pennsylvania (PA)
University of Pittsburgh (PA)

Pharmacy

Butler University (IN)
Drake University (IA)
Duquesne University (PA)
Ohio Northern University (OH)
Purdue University (IN)
Rutgers University (NJ)
University of Connecticut (CT)
University of Georgia (GA)
University of Kansas (KS)
University of Pittsburgh (PA)

Philosophy

Colgate University (NY)
College of the Holy Cross (MA)
Fordham University (NY)
Indiana University (IN)
Princeton University (NJ)
Reed College (OR)
St. Louis University (MO)
Trinity College (CT)
University of Arizona (AZ)
University of California at Berkeley (CA)
University of Chicago (IL)
University of Notre Dame (IN)
University of Pennsylvania (PA)
University of Pittsburgh (PA)
University of the South (TN)

Wheaton College (IL)
Yale University (CT)

Physical Education

Ithaca College (NY)
Michigan State University (MI)
Pennsylvania State University (PA)
Purdue University (IN)
Springfield College (MA)
University of California at Santa
    Barbara (CA)
University of Colorado (CO)
University of Iowa (IA)
University of Texas (TX)
Washington State University (WA)

Physical Therapy

Boston University (MA)
Ithaca College (NY)
Marquette University (WI)
Northeastern University (MA)
Ohio University (OH)
Saint Louis University (MO)
Temple University (PA)
University of California at
    San Francisco (CA)
University of Connecticut (CT)
University of Evansville (IN)
University of Florida (FL)
University of Pittsburgh (PA)
University of Wisconsin (WI)

Physics

Agnes Scott College (GA)
Albion College (MI)
California Institute of Technology (CA)
Case Western Reserve University (OH)
Franklin and Marshall College (PA)
Georgia Institute of Technology (GA)
Grinnell College (IA)

Harvey Mudd College (CA)

Massachusetts Institute of Technology (MA)

Princeton University (NJ)

Rensselaer Polytechnic Institute (NY)

Rhodes College (TN)

University of California at Berkeley (CA)

University of Chicago (IL)

University of Colorado (CO)

University of Maryland (MD)

Ursinus College (PA)

Worcester Polytechnic Institute (MA)

Pre-Law

Centre College (KY)

Columbia University (NY)

Duke University (NC)

Emory University (GA)

George Washington University (DC)

Georgetown University (DC)

Hendrix College (AR)

Princeton University (NJ)

University of Virginia (VA)

Washington and Lee University (VA)

Pre-Med

Brandeis University (MA)

Case Western Reserve University (OH)

Emory University (GA)

Franklin and Marshall College (PA)

Hendrix College (AR)

Johns Hopkins University (MD)

Stanford University (CA)

University of Michigan (MI)

University of Notre Dame (IN)

University of Rochester (NY)

Ursinus College (PA)

Vanderbilt University (TN)

Washington and Jefferson College (PA)

Psychology

Brandeis College (MA)

Bucknell University (PA)

Clark University (MA)

Cornell College (IA)

Cornell University (NY)

Duke University (NC)

Duquesne University (PA)

Emory University (GA)

Gettysburg College (PA)

Hollins College (VA)

Hope College (MI)

Lafayette College (PA)

New College of the University of South Florida (FL)

Occidental College (CA)

Ohio Wesleyan University (OH)

Stanford University (CA)

Sweet Briar College (VA)

University of California at Los Angeles (CA)

University of California at Santa Cruz (CA)

University of Oregon (OR)

Wake Forest University (NC)

Williams College (MA)

Religious Studies

Brown University (RI)

Catholic University (DC)

Dartmouth College (NH)

Davidson College (NC)

Duke University (NC)

Fordham University (NY)

Georgetown University (DC)

Kenyon College (OH)

Princeton University (NJ)

University of Chicago (IL)

University of Notre Dame (IN)

University of Virginia (VA)

Wake Forest University (NC)

Sociology

Beloit College (WI)
Bryn Mawr College (PA)
Columbia University (NY)
Lewis and Clark University (OR)
Spelman College (GA)
St. Lawrence University (NY)
University of California at Los Angeles (CA)
University of Chicago (IL)
University of Michigan (MI)
University of North Carolina at Chapel Hill (NC)
Whitman College (WA)

Theatre/Drama

Carnegie Mellon University (PA)
Drew University (NJ)
Florida State University (FL)

Fordham University (NY)
Hanover College (IN)
Indiana University (IN)
New York University (NY)
Northwestern University (IL)
Ohio University (OH)
Otterbein College (OH)
The Juilliard School (NY)
University of California at Los Angeles (CA)
University of Evansville (IN)
Vassar College (NY)
Yale University (CT)

Veterinary Medicine

Auburn (AL)
Colorado State University (CO)
Texas A&M University (TX)

SPECIAL CATEGORIES

COLLEGES WITH BEAUTIFUL CAMPUSES

Bucknell University (PA)
Colby College (ME)
Colgate University (NY)
Dartmouth College (NH)
Denison University (OH)
Drew University (NJ)
Duke University (NC)

Hendrix College (AR)
Pepperdine University (CA)
Princeton University (NJ)
Sweet Briar College (VA)
University of Colorado (CO)
University of Notre Dame (IN)
Wellesley College (MA)

COLLEGES WITH GREAT RESIDENCE HALLS

Bowdoin College (ME)
Bryn Mawr College (PA)
Bucknell University (PA)
Colorado College (CO)
Haverford College (PA)
Pepperdine University (CA)
Trinity University (TX)
University of Vermont (VT)

COLLEGES WITH THE MOST STUDIOUS STUDENTS

Bates College (ME)
Bryn Mawr College (PA)
Bucknell University (PA)
California Institute of Technology (CA)
Cornell University (NY)
Harvey Mudd College (CA)
Massachusetts Institute of Technology (MA)
Reed College (OR)
Swarthmore College (PA)
University of Chicago (IL)

COLLEGES WITH THE FRIENDLIEST STUDENTS

Colorado College (CO)
Cornell College (IA)
Hanover College (IN)
Loyola Marymount University (CA)
Morehouse College (GA)
Ripon College (WI)
Southwestern University (TX)
Sweet Briar College (VA)

Trinity University (TX)
University of Colorado (CO)
Wabash College (IN)
Whitman College (WA)

COLLEGES WITH MANY INTERNATIONAL STUDENTS

American University (DC)
Boston University (MA)
Massachusetts Institute of Technology (MA)
University of Houston (TX)
University of Miami (FL)
University of San Francisco (CA)
University of Southern California (CA)
University of Texas (TX)
University of Wisconsin (WI)

COLLEGES WITH STUDENTS WHO SEEM VERY HAPPY

Colby College (ME)
Colgate University (NY)
College of Wooster (OH)
Grinnell College (IA)
Hanover College (IN)
Hobart and William Smith Colleges (NY)
Lawrence University (WI)
Ripon College (WI)
Rollins College (FL)
University of Colorado (CO)
University of the South (TN)

COLLEGES THAT SEEM SAFER THAN MOST

Carleton College (MN)
Colby College (ME)
Colgate College (NY)
Furman University (SC)
Hendrix College (AR)
Lawrence University (WI)
Sweet Briar College (VA)
University of the South (TN)
Washington and Lee University (VA)
Whitman College (WA)
Williams College (MA)

COLLEGES WITH VERY DIVERSE STUDENT BODIES

American University (DC)
Antioch College (OH)
Bard College (NY)
Boston University (MA)
Brown University (RI)
Earlham College (IN)
George Washington University (DC)
New York University (NY)
Oberlin College (OH)
Reed College (OR)
University of Chicago (IL)
Wesleyan University (CT)

COLLEGES WITH POLITICALLY CONSERVATIVE STUDENT BODIES

Baylor University (TX)
Brigham Young University (UT)
Calvin College (MI)

Dartmouth College (NH)
Grove City College (PA)
Hampden-Sydney College (VA)
Hillsdale College (MI)
University of Notre Dame (IN)
University of the South (TN)
Wabash College (IN)

COLLEGES WITH POLITCALLY LIBERAL STUDENT BODIES

Bard College (NY)
Columbia University (NY)
Grinnell College (IA)
Hampshire College (MA)
Harvard University (MA)
Oberlin College (OH)
Reed College (OR)
Stanford University (CA)
University of Chicago (IL)
Wesleyan University (CT)
Whitman College (WA)

COLLEGES WITH PROFESSORS WHO LOVE TO TEACH

Bucknell University (PA)
Cornell College (IA)
Dartmouth College (NH)
Davidson College (NC)
Hendrix College (AR)
Sweet Briar College (VA)
University of the South (TN)
Wabash College (IN)
Williams College (MA)

COLLEGES WITH OUTSTANDING OUTDOOR PROGRAMS

Bowdoin College (ME)
Colby College (ME)
Colorado State University (CO)
Skidmore College (NY)
St. Lawrence University (NY)
University of California at Santa Cruz (CA)
University of Oregon (OR)
University of the South (TN)
University of Vermont (VT)
Whitman College (WA)
Williams College (MA)

COLLEGES WITH VERY ACTIVE FRATERNITY AND SORORITY SYSTEMS

Denison University (OH)
Indiana University (IN)
Lehigh University (PA)
Purdue University (IN)
Southern Methodist University (TX)
University of Georgia (GA)
University of Michigan (MI)
University of Virginia (VA)
Vanderbilt University (TN)
Washington and Lee University (VA)

COLLEGES WITH VERY GOOD PROGRAMS FOR STUDENTS WITH DIFFERENT LEARNING STYLES

Adelphi College (NY)
Bradford College (MA)
Curry College (MA)

Landmark College (VT)
Loras College (IA)
Muskingum College (OH)
Westminster College (MO)

COLLEGES THAT ARE PERSONAL FAVORITES

South

Davidson College (NC). Excellent academic programs, fine facilities, very talented student body.

Emory University (GA). Extensive facility, diverse student body, outstanding faculty, wonderful location in Atlanta.

Hampden-Sydney College (VA). Extensive traditions; truly dedicated to the academic, personal, and social development of men.

Hendrix College (AR). One of the best-kept secrets in higher education in terms of quality students and faculty, beautiful campus and excellent facilities.

Morehouse College (GA). Outstanding tradition of excellence in higher education, outstanding location, "brother" college to Spelman College.

Sweet Briar College (VA). Outstanding women's college that delivers on high expectations of students and parents.

University of the South (TN). Talented and caring faculty, excellent student body, comfortable and expansive campus.

University of Virginia (VA). Beautiful campus, dedicated faculty, extensive course offerings, strong sense of community for a state university.

Vanderbilt University (TN). Beautiful campus, dedicated faculty, extensive facilities, intellectual vision.

Wake Forest University (NC). Outstanding facilities, talented faculty, gifted and involved student body.

Washington and Lee University (VA). Strong sense of social and academic community, dedication to honor principle, impressive traditions.

East

Boston College (MA). Outstanding location, extensive academic and athletic opportunities, caring and talented faculty.

Bowdoin College (ME). Great balance of outstanding academic programs, good athletic program, nice college town environment.

Bucknell University (PA). Outstanding facilities, extraordinarily loyal student body, impressive academic opportunities.

Colby College (ME). Caring and talented faculty, impressive campus, extensive student and faculty relationships.

Colgate University (NY). Outstanding faculty, extensive and beautiful campus, very involved student body.

Dartmouth College (NH). Excellent academic environment, outstanding athletic program, extensive facilities, beautiful campus. (I'm a bit biased. Dartmouth is my alma mater.)

Dickinson College (PA). Historic campus, active and bright students, internationally focused academic program.

Drew University (NJ). Fine academic program, beautiful campus, only 40 miles from New York City.

Gettysburg College (PA). Active, talented, and happy students; accessible faculty; beautiful and historic location.

Johns Hopkins University (MD). Super academic programs, exceptionally bright and dedicated students, outstanding preprofessional programs.

Princeton University (NJ). Striking campus, outstanding facilities, faculty and student relationship is exceptional.

Syracuse University (NY). Diverse and loyal student body, extensive facilities, numerous academic options.

University of Pennsylvania (PA). Urban environment, extraordinary academic options, talented and motivated students.

University of Rochester (NY). Wonderful facilities, talented faculty, extensive internship opportunities.

Wellesley College (MA). Super-talented student body, beautiful campus, devoted faculty, wonderful facilities.

Williams College (MA). Ultimate small college town, talented and caring faculty, gifted student body.

Midwest

College of Wooster (OH). Caring students and faculty, impressive facilities, satisfied students and parents.

Cornell College (IA). Innovative academic program of one-course-at-a-time, caring faculty, very active students.

Indiana University (IN). Many exceptional academic programs, outstanding facilities, dedicated graduates.

Lawrence University (WI). Unusual blend of liberal and fine arts programs, incredible faculty, very talented students.

Macalester College (MN). Impressive facilities, diverse student body, great urbanish location.

Marquette University (WI). Positive blend of strong academic program with community service focus, well located in an urban environment.

Miami University (OH). State university with excellent blend of academic and extracurricular opportunities, impressive facilities.

Northwestern University (IL). Outstanding academic programs, impressive campus, talented student body who believe institution delivers on promises.

Ripon College (WI). Very caring and talented faculty who truly enjoy teaching, individuals respected for many talents.

University of Chicago (IL). High-powered faculty, student body with real thirst for learning, extensive facilities.

University of Notre Dame (IN). Unmatched balance of academics, athletics, and community service; strikingly beautiful campus; special school spirit.

Wabash College (IN). Extraordinary student and faculty relationships, loyal student body, a place where being a "Gentleman" is expected and respected.

West

Claremont McKenna College (CA). Extraordinary relationship between faculty and students, centrally located to other Claremont Colleges, strong preprofessional programs.

Colorado College (CO). Progressive student body, wonderful location, unique block academic program.

Loyola Marymount University (CA). Diverse and talented student body, wholesome environment, impressive facilities.

Occidental College (CA). Strong academic programs, caring and talented faculty, impressive campus.

Pepperdine University (CA). Beautiful location, impressive facilities, good academic programs.

Rice University (TX). Exceptional academic program and students, low cost, wonderful facilities.

Stanford University (CA). Excellence in many areas, strong athletic programs, extensive campus.

Trinity College (TX). Outstanding facilities, excellent faculty, student body that truly wants to learn.

University of Colorado at Boulder (CO). Unbelievable location at the foot of the Rockies, extensive course offerings, extensive extracurricular opportunities.

University of Oregon (OR). Strong academic programs, beautiful campus, outdoors-oriented.

Whitman College (WA). Comfortable pace of life, excellent faculty, friendly student body, progressive environment.